WRITTEN BY LATRE'

The 42 Laws Of Kindness

First published by Midnite Dakota Publishing 2025

Copyright © 2025 by Written By LaTre'

All rights reserved. No part of this publication may be reproduced, stored or transmitted in any form or by any means, electronic, mechanical, photocopying, recording, scanning, or otherwise without written permission from the publisher. It is illegal to copy this book, post it to a website, or distribute it by any other means without permission.

First edition

ISBN: 979-8-9915180-2-4

This book was professionally typeset on Reedsy. Find out more at reedsy.com

Contents

Foreword	v
Acknowledgments	vi
Law 1	1
Law 2	4
Law 3	8
Law 4	12
Law 5	17
Law 6	21
Law 7	26
Law 8	30
Law 9	34
Law 10	39
Law 11	43
Law 12	47
Law 13	52
Law 14	56
Law 15	60
Law 16	65
Law 17	69
Law 18	73
Law 19	78
Law 20	82
Law 21	87
Law 22	92

Law 23	96
Law 24	101
Law 25	105
Law 26	110
Law 27	115
Law 28	120
Law 29	124
Law 30	129
Law 31	134
Law 32	139
Law 33	144
Law 34	148
Law 35	153
Law 36	158
Law 37	162
Law 38	167
Law 39	171
Law 40	176
Law 41	181
Law 42	186
Be Kind, Be Kind, Be Kind!	191

Foreword

There are three ways to ultimate success.
   The first way is to be kind.
   The second way is to be kind.
   The third way is to be kind."
   — Fred Rogers

Acknowledgments

Through trail and tribulation I have gained my knowledge. Through pain and tears I have tested it. Through success and euphoria I have proven it. Through time and love I teach you.

Law 1

Kindness Is Control

There is a kind of evening that calms you the moment the door closes behind you. The air is cool outside, the lights are soft inside, and a gentle kettle begins to hum. That is what real control feels like. Not a boil, not a flare, simply a steady warmth that makes a room kinder just by being there. Kindness lives at that temperature. It is not the absence of strength. It is strength that knows its own heat and uses only what is needed.

Control begins in small choices. The way you place your voice on the table as neatly as a linen napkin. The way you breathe as if there is time, because there is. The way your eyes rest not on the sharp edges of a moment, but on the people who are trying, even when they are not at their best. When you lead with that calm, you do not meet chaos on its terms. You invite it to meet you on yours.

In a text thread that starts to tilt. In traffic when another driver forgets there are hearts in the cars as well as engines. A kind person does not pretend friction is imaginary. A kind person lowers the heat so wisdom can speak. Lowering the heat is not silence. It is curation. Keep what serves the moment, set the rest aside until there is space for it.

Some people will reach for performance. They will want volume, speed, a quick score. Do not audition. Keep your tone even. Answer the question that matters, not the one meant to scrape. If the scraping continues, you can step back with grace. We can continue when respect returns. There is no anger in that sentence. There is a door, and it is open to better behavior.

Kindness keeps time. It knows certain conversations belong to later, the way some sauces prefer a slow evening to a hurried noon. Choosing later is not avoidance. It is letting truth arrive dressed properly. It protects outcomes. It also protects you. Your peace is a resource. Treat it the way you treat flour and light. Measure it, use what is needed, save enough for tomorrow.

Even in sharper places, the same rule holds. The calmest person becomes the center of gravity. Your steadiness says, I will not make a new mess to clean an old one. Your steadiness says, I see the future and I would like it intact. People soften, not because they lost, but because you gave them a way to win without harm.

Control is not a trick of words. It is a practice of the body. Shoulders down. Jaw soft. Hands open. Feet steady as if you were standing on a favorite kitchen mat. Breathe in to a count of five, breathe out to a count of five. Let your words arrive like place cards, each with a purpose. If the room rises, lower. If the room cools, warm. Keep your compass. Keep your kindness.

Boundaries belong in beautiful rooms. If voices turn sharp twice, pause the exchange. If safety feels uncertain, step away and choose a better moment. If a conversation begins to walk in circles, set it down and put a time on the clock for a cleaner attempt. Afterward, write what was agreed so memory does not wander. If the same pattern returns, reduce access, then release it if you must. A tidy exit is a gift to both of you.

When the dishes are drying, notice how control felt. Not rigid. Not brittle. More like a well made blanket that holds shape and warmth at once. That is what you are building. A way of moving through the world that keeps you composed and keeps others safe near you. People remember this. They remember the flavor of your presence long after the words fade. They remember that you made a place where they could calm down and choose better.

Kindness is control because it guides a room to its best self. It steadies the hand that would otherwise shake. It chooses a gentle word that still tells the truth. It knows that power without care breaks things, and that care without power saves nothing. So it carries both, one in each hand, and sets a table where even difficult moments can be served with dignity.

Before you turn the page, let the kettle hum once more. Breathe in, breathe out, and offer yourself one quiet promise. I will be the warm center in a cold moment. I will keep the flame steady. My peace is my power, and I will share it wisely.

Law 2

Energy Bows to Intention

Every space you enter listens to you before anyone does. Not to your words first, but to what you mean. Intention is a quiet current. It shapes how your energy moves across a room, through a message, and into the heart of another person. When your intention is clean, your energy becomes clear. People relax. Doors ease open. Even hard moments soften because they can feel you are here to help and not to harm.

Think of water poured into a glass. The water takes the shape it is given. Energy does the same thing with intention. If your intention is to protect peace, your energy arrives organized and calm. If your intention is to prove someone wrong, your energy arrives sharp even when your voice sounds sweet. People may not be able to explain why they do not trust a sentence, but they can feel the curve underneath it.

This law does not ask you to perform. It asks you to get honest. Before you send the text or walk into the meeting, pause for one breath and name your real aim. I want repair. I want clarity. I want to learn. If the answer is I want to win the moment, do not judge yourself. Name it, then choose a better aim and let your tone line up with it.

At home, intention can change the shape of an entire evening. You can ask a child to clean a room with the intention to teach skill, and the request will sound patient and simple. You can ask the same thing with the intention to discharge your stress, and it will land like a storm. The words may be nearly the same. The energy is not. Children feel this difference faster than adults do. So do partners.

At work, your intention writes the first draft of every outcome. Go into a tough conversation with the intention to understand and you will ask real questions. You will wait for the full answer. You will hear the piece that is your responsibility and you will accept it without a speech. Go in with the intention to defend your image and you will miss the path to a solution that would have saved everyone time and cost. The work will show your intention in the end. It is wiser to choose it on purpose at the start.

Intention is not magic, but it is direction. When your intention is steady, your actions begin to line up without strain. You pick warmer words. You select a kinder time to bring a hard topic. You stop sending messages that could have been a thoughtful call. You remove the extra glitter from your sentence when you notice it is there to impress rather than to help. This alignment is what people feel. That feeling turns into trust.

Your body carries intention too. It shows in how you breathe and hold your shoulders. It shows in whether you look at a person or at the door behind them. Train your body to match your aim. Sit back an inch. Unclench your jaw. Let your hands rest where they can be seen. These small choices tell another nervous system that you mean safety. Often that is all a tense moment needs.

There will be times when you are tired, hurt, or afraid. In those hours your energy will try to follow fear. Bring it back with a simple practice. Name the room. Name the aim. Name one step that honors both. For example. Kitchen. Respect. Ask for a pause and set a time to finish this talk after we eat. Or. Team check in. Clarity. Show the problem in three lines and propose the next test. Intention becomes visible through small, plain actions.

Kindness does not mean you agree with everything or accept harm. It means you hold an intention that no one loses their dignity, including you. If you must leave, you can leave with that intention. You can say I wish you well and I am stepping away. Your energy will leave a clean line where you stood. People remember that kind of exit long after the details fade.

Language helps you carry this law. Keep a few sentences ready that declare your aim in the moment. I am here to understand. I would like a fair plan for both of us. I want to fix what is in my control. May I start again. These phrases steady you and signal to others that you are not here to score points. You are here to make something better.

If you wonder whether your intention is getting through, watch what follows your words. Do faces soften. Do shoulders drop. Does the next person tell the truth more easily. That is the bow. Energy bends toward the purpose you set. When the result is noise and confusion, return to the start. Reset the aim. Speak less. Act with care. Intention is not a speech. It is a line you hold.

End this chapter with a brief check you can use today. Before your next important exchange, write one sentence in your notes. My intention is to create peace and progress. Then choose one action that proves it. Pour water. Ask the clear question. Offer a path forward. When your intention is chosen with care, energy follows. The room feels it. The work shows it. And your life begins to move in the direction you meant all along.

Law 3

Mercy Is Measured Strength

Mercy is not a soft spot. It is a steady hand. It knows when to release a weight and when to keep a boundary. It keeps your spirit from hardening, and it keeps your life from breaking. Mercy is strength because it requires control. You choose your response instead of letting injury choose it for you.

Think of mercy as warm light through a window. It does not erase winter. It makes the room livable while you handle what must be handled. When someone harms you, mercy helps you see the whole picture. The person, the pattern, the impact, and the next right step. Sometimes the next step is forgiveness. Sometimes it is distance. Often it is both.

Forgiveness and reconciliation are not the same. Forgiveness frees your heart. Reconciliation rebuilds trust. Forgiveness can be offered by one person. Reconciliation needs two who are willing to repair. Mercy understands this difference. It releases bitterness without returning to a door that should remain closed.

Mercy also respects consequence. If a rule was broken at home, mercy asks for repair. The pillowcase that tore is sewn. The tone that crossed a line is owned and corrected. The teenager returns the borrowed item and says the real words. I took this without asking. I want to make it right. Mercy holds the line and removes the shame that keeps people stuck. Everyone learns and the house stays kind.

At work, mercy looks like clarity without humiliation. You name what missed. You offer the path to fix it. You leave a person's dignity intact so they have room to grow. The email does not include sarcasm. The meeting does not become a show. Progress becomes the proof that you handled the moment with wisdom.

With friends, mercy is honest about capacity. You love them and you also notice when your energy is running thin. You do not promise a long talk if what you have is ten minutes. You do not say yes to a project you cannot carry. Mercy tells the truth early. It stops resentment from forming. It frees you to show up with a full heart in the places you can.

There is also mercy for yourself. You are not a machine. You will forget. You will respond poorly. You will learn in public sometimes. Offer yourself the same tone you offer a child who is trying again. Speak to yourself in clear and kind sentences. I made a mistake. I can repair it. Here is the next small step. Self mercy is not an excuse. It is the fuel that keeps you going.

Mercy is measured. That means it is specific to the moment. It notices the person's history. It notices your history with them. It notices what safety requires. Then it chooses the smallest strong response that keeps everyone human. You do not need a speech when a sentence will do. You do not need a punishment when a repair will teach more.

Your body can help you choose mercy. When the pulse runs fast, take one slow breath. Place a palm flat on a table. Feel the surface that holds you. Name what you want to protect. Peace. Respect. Time. Once your body settles, your words will carry less heat and more clarity. This is how strength feels when it is calm.

There is a myth that mercy means you must let people keep taking. Mercy is not permission. It is a clean no when a no is needed. It is a change of access when trust is not safe. It is a quiet exit when a room refuses respect. You can wish someone well and still keep your distance. That is mercy for both of you.

If you need language for a hard moment, keep a few lines ready. I want a good outcome for both of us. Here is what happened and here is how it landed. Here is what I can offer. Here is what I need. I am choosing to forgive and I am also choosing a boundary. These sentences are simple tools. They set the tone and the limits at the same time.

Mercy has timing. You do not need to decide everything the minute pain arrives. You can say I need a little time to think so I can respond well. You can step outside. You can drink water. You can return when you are able to speak from values rather than from shock. A delayed response that is thoughtful is stronger than a quick answer that adds harm.

There will be days when mercy feels costly. You may worry that people will mistake your kindness for weakness. The truth is the opposite. People sense when you could cut and choose not to. They sense when you tell the truth without trying to wound. They feel safer near you because you do not use power to embarrass. You use it to stabilize.

Let the results guide you. After a merciful choice, do you sleep better. Do conversations move forward. Does the home or the team feel calmer. If yes, you chose well. If no, adjust the measure. Add firmer boundaries next time. Ask for accountability in writing. Shorten the leash on deadlines. Mercy learns. It gets more precise with practice.

Close this chapter with one small practice. Think of a person who made a real mistake that still bothers you. Write one sentence that names the impact. Write one sentence that states the boundary. Write one sentence that offers a path for repair. Keep it short and kind. If action is wise, send it. If the matter is old and finished, release it. Place your hand on your heart and say, I choose my peace.

Mercy is measured strength. It protects your softness without letting people trample it. It clears your spirit so you can live light and direct. It keeps relationships honest. It keeps homes calm. It keeps teams healthy. Practice it in your words, in your timing, and in your exits. Your life will carry a quiet authority that others can trust.

Law 4

Stillness Commands Respect

Stillness is not the absence of sound. It is the decision to move from a steady center. It is a posture that tells the room you are not available for chaos. When you practice stillness, you do not shrink. You become clear. People feel the difference right away. Voices lower. Choices get simpler. Respect rises because steadiness is rare.

Think of a calm lake at sunrise. The surface looks quiet, yet beneath it there is depth and life. That is the nature of stillness. You are not doing nothing. You are holding your ground with care. You are listening for what matters. You are giving wisdom a chance to reach you before emotion does.

Many of us were taught to answer quickly. We try to win the moment with speed. Stillness chooses timing instead of speed. A pause gives your mind room to line up with your values. A short breath can prevent a long mess. The pause is not a stall. It is leadership. You are telling your nervous system that you are safe to think.

Stillness does not mean silence at all costs. It means you stop matching the loudest energy in the room. If someone raises their voice, you do not match it. If a message arrives with pressure, you do not reply with pressure. You set the temperature instead of catching it. That is what earns respect. You are useful because you are not swept away.

At home, stillness can turn a heated moment into a useful one. Picture a child who spills something and then lies about it. Your first impulse might be a lecture. Instead, stand still for a count of three and look at the floor rather than the child. Name what is true without heat. The juice is on the rug. We will clean it. Tell me what happened. The room will feel your steadiness and follow it.

At work, a leader who practices stillness becomes the person others seek when things feel messy. In a tough meeting, you can say a quiet sentence that slows the spin. Let us write the facts on the board. Here is the decision we need by noon. Here is what we do know. Here is what we do not know. The team sees that your calm is not passive. It is active guidance.

Stillness also protects your dignity. When someone tries to provoke you, they are hoping you will play their game. They want you to perform. You can choose stillness instead. Sit back an inch. Unclench your jaw. Place your feet flat. Speak one simple line. I hear you. I will respond after I think. Your calm signals that you own yourself.

Your body can be trained for this. Start with a practice that takes less than one minute. Inhale through your nose for four counts. Hold for four. Exhale for six. Do it three times before you speak. The longer exhale tells your body that you are safe. Your voice will come out warmer and steadier. People listen to a warm steady voice.

Stillness is not a mask for fear. It is a commitment to clarity. You can be firm within it. You can say no. You can set limits. You can leave. The difference is that you do these things without the extra noise that invites a fight. Stillness turns boundaries into simple facts. I will not continue this conversation while I am being interrupted. I am happy to talk when we can both listen.

If you grew up in a house where the loudest person always won, stillness may feel strange at first. That is normal. You are changing a pattern. Begin with low stakes moments. When the line is slow, stand comfortably and relax your face rather than sighing. When a message frustrates you, draft a reply then read it aloud in a calm voice. If it sounds like a storm, do not send it. Clean it up and remove any extra heat.

Stillness helps you notice what is yours to carry and what is not. When you are calm you can sort the pile. This is my part. This is their part. This is the part that belongs to time. Respect often follows people who can make that kind of distinction. You save effort. You do not crowd the space. You choose the essential action and release the rest.

There will be moments when someone mistakes your stillness

for indifference. You can correct that without losing your center. Say one clear sentence with eye contact. I care about this very much. I am choosing careful words so we can solve it. That sentence changes how your quiet is read. Now it sounds like responsibility instead of distance.

Keep a few tools nearby to support this law. Write short phrases you can use when your heart starts to rush. I want to understand. Let me write this down. Give me a minute and I will answer clearly. I am going to step away and return at two. These lines protect your pace and your quality. They also teach others that you do not trade clarity for speed.

The point of stillness is not to impress anyone. The point is to move in a way that honors truth and protects dignity. When you model that, people adjust. Friends feel safer speaking honestly. Children learn to settle themselves. Colleagues bring you real information because they know you will not make a scene. Respect grows in the soil of steady presence.

Close with a practice you can try today. Choose one recurring moment that tends to pull you into reactivity. The doorbell. A certain name in your inbox. A topic at dinner. Decide on a script and a breath before it happens again. When it comes, keep your shoulders down, breathe once slowly, and use the script. Repeat this for one week. Watch what shifts.

Stillness commands respect because it is power that does not need to perform. It is a quiet anchor that steadies you and anyone near you. When you carry it, your choices get cleaner, your words land softer, and your life moves with more grace.

Keep the center and let everything else take its right size.

Law 5

Generosity Multiplies What You Keep

Generosity is not about losing. It is about flow. When you open your hand, you do not end up empty. You create movement through your life, and movement brings return. Sometimes the return is money. Often it is peace, clarity, and good timing. People remember how you made things easier. The world remembers too.

There is a difference between generosity and pleasing. Pleasing spends your energy to avoid discomfort. Generosity invests your energy to create value. One drains. The other plants. When you give with a clean heart and a clear boundary, you keep your dignity and you raise the room.

Start with the simplest form of generosity. Attention. Most people feel starved for it. Put your phone down when someone speaks. Look at them. Let them finish. Ask one clean question. What would help most right now. That moment costs almost nothing and changes the air. Attention tells a person they matter, and people who feel seen behave better.

Generosity also looks like clarity. Share the map. If you know a process that saves twenty minutes, teach it. If you have a contact who could help, make the introduction with care. At work this can feel risky. You may worry that someone will pass you. The truth is the opposite. People who multiply clarity become the ones others trust with bigger work.

Credit is public generosity. Say names when you win. Put the person who did the heavy lift first in the email. If a partner made the idea better, tell the story that way. Credit does not shrink you. It builds a community that wants to build with you again. Your own name grows because it lives in good company.

Money can be a tool for generosity, but it is not the only one. Some people have time. Some have skill. Some have networks. Give from what is in your hand. A well written paragraph can be worth more than a large purchase. A babysitting hour can be priceless to a tired parent. A ride to an appointment can be a kindness that fixes a week.

Generosity requires boundaries so it can stay pure. Without them, it turns into resentment. Name what you can offer and by when. I can review this by Friday. I can watch the kids until three. I can lend this tool if it is back tomorrow. Clear edges protect the gift and the giver. When you cannot give, say so early and kind. I am not able to do that. Here are two options that may help. That sentence keeps your heart open without creating a debt you cannot pay.

Your body can practice generosity too. Soften your face when you greet someone. Keep your hands where they can be seen. Offer a calm tone. These signals tell another nervous system that you mean safety. People relax near safety. Deals get easier. Home becomes lighter.

There is a form of generosity that seems small but matters. Remove friction. Hold the door. Label the container. Put the tool back where it belongs. Write the step by step once so the next person can move without asking you. These simple acts repay you every single time. They build a culture that carries weight together.

What about people who take advantage. They exist. This law does not ask you to fund their habits. It asks you to keep your spirit generous while you stay wise. You can be kind and still say no. You can wish someone well and still choose distance. You can give only through channels that protect both sides, like written agreements or office hours or a clear limit on favors each month. Wisdom keeps your river clean.

If you have lived with scarcity, generosity can feel unsafe. Try a small practice that does not risk your stability. Choose one area for seven days. Time. Praise. Advice. Each day, give a small gift that fits your life. Ten minutes to help a neighbor carry groceries. One paragraph of specific thanks to a teammate. One clean resource for a person who is stuck. Watch for the returns. They may not come from the same person. They often arrive as ease in an unrelated part of your life. That is how flow works.

Generosity also helps you forgive. When you bless someone

in your mind, even lightly, your own spirit lifts. The knot in your chest loosens. You move with more room. This does not remove consequence. It removes the poison that consequence leaves behind. You get your energy back so you can build again.

Language can keep your giving clean. Try lines like these. I can offer this, not that. Here is what I know, and here is what I do not know. I am happy to help if we agree on this plan. Thank you for the part you did. Each sentence gives without creating confusion. Clarity is a gift.

In your home, make generosity visible and ordinary. Keep a small basket by the door for give away items. Teach children to return borrowed things better than they received them. At dinner, ask everyone to share one kindness they gave today. Do not take a bow. Just name it. The practice grows roots.

In your work, set a rhythm. One introduction a week. One resource shared. One note of credit. Put it on your calendar. Small rhythms become large rivers. Over time your name will carry a reputation that protects you more than any secret could.

Close with a simple test you can use any time. Before you give, ask two questions. Is my intention clean. Are my boundaries clear. If both are yes, go ahead. If either is no, pause and adjust. Then give what you can without strings. The open hand never stays empty. What you send into the world returns as trust, as timing, and as a life that keeps moving. Generosity multiplies what you keep.

Law 6

The Heart Has Its Own Logic

There is a kind of knowing that does not arrive through debate. It shows up as a pull in your chest, a soft yes, or a steady no. The mind asks for proof. The heart offers direction. When you honor that direction with clear action, kindness becomes precise. You stop trying to win arguments and start choosing the most human path that still protects what matters.

Heart logic is not fantasy. It is a form of pattern recognition built from memory, values, and lived experience. It notices tone before it catches words. It hears what is missing as clearly as what is said. It feels the cost of a choice on the people in the room. Where the mind tries to control, the heart tries to connect. You need both. The heart points to the truth. The mind builds the plan.

At home, the heart often sees the quickest way back to peace. A child is melting down. Your head wants reasons and rules. Your heart knows to sit on the floor, open your arms, and breathe with them until the wave passes. After calm returns, the lesson will land. Presence first. Instruction second. This order keeps dignity intact for everyone.

With a partner, heart logic protects closeness without sacrificing clarity. It helps you ask what lives underneath the loud part. Are you tired or are you feeling unseen. Do you need a fix or do you need company. The right question lowers the temperature because it proves you are aiming for understanding rather than a win. The mind can then help you choose the next step.

At work, the heart is useful when decisions involve trust. Data may point to a choice that looks fast but breaks relationships. The heart warns you about the long tail. It asks whether the plan honors the people who must carry it. You can still move quickly. You simply choose a path that gets you speed without tearing the fabric of the team. Invite one more voice that will be affected. Write the promise you are making in plain language. If it still feels right, proceed.

Your body delivers the heart's messages first. Learn its signals. Tight jaw means you are about to push when you should pause. Warmth in the chest means you have found the right fit. A sinking feeling means your values are about to be traded for convenience. When a signal arrives, do a short check. What is my real intention. What outcome protects both truth and dignity. What is the smallest next step that honors both. Then act on that step within the hour.

Heart logic is not the same as rescuing. It will ask you to set boundaries so love can stay clean. Sometimes the kindest thing you can say is no. Sometimes the kindest move is distance. You can keep a soft heart while you guard your energy. You can wish someone well while you choose not to reopen a door that history tells you is unsafe. The heart is tender and it is not foolish.

There will be days when the heart asks for something that does not make sense to your schedule. Call your elder now. Bring soup to that neighbor. Send the honest thank you. Write the apology. These small acts are not random. They build a life where people feel cared for and where you can also sleep at night. The return shows up as timing that seems lucky and rooms that welcome you.

Language helps the heart speak in places where logic tries to rule. Keep a few lines ready that carry both care and clarity. I hear you and I want to understand. Here is what I can offer today. I respect your view and I have to choose a different path. Thank you for telling me the truth. These sentences do not try to impress. They connect and direct.

Beware of sentimentality that dresses up avoidance. If your heart is telling you to keep forgiving while harm continues, check again. Ask two questions. Is this act still protecting dignity, including mine. Is there a clear boundary and a path to repair. If either answer is no, let your kindness take the form of limits and distance. The heart's logic serves life, not repetition of pain.

Practice helps this law become reliable. Try a daily two minute ritual. Sit with your feet on the floor. Put a hand on your chest. Breathe in for four and out for six. Ask one question. What is the honest move that would bring more peace today. Do not wait for poetry. Listen for a simple instruction. Drink water. Tell the truth to that person. Put your phone away during dinner. Then do it. The heart speaks more often when it learns you will act.

You can also bring the heart into group decisions without sounding vague. Name the facts in writing. Add one line for care. Here is what we know. Here is what we do not know. Here is the impact on people if we are wrong. Here is how we will check in after the change. That single care line is heart logic turned into a practical guardrail.

If you feel torn between head and heart, try this approach. Give the mind five minutes to list options. Give the heart one minute to choose the one that honors truth and dignity. Then ask the mind to build the steps. You are not throwing away intelligence. You are aiming it where the heart points.

Close with a test you can use in any room. After you speak or act, watch what happens to the energy around you. Do shoulders drop. Do people tell more truth. Do you feel steady in your own body. That is how you know the heart was guiding and not fear. When the result is noise or a tight chest, return to center. Ask for a reset. Choose a kinder line. Try again.

The heart has its own logic. It leads you toward what is alive and asks you to protect it with skill. Let it set the aim. Let the mind build the road. When the two work together, kindness stops being a performance and becomes a way of moving through the world that holds its shape under pressure. You will be easier to trust. You will waste less time. And the rooms you touch will feel more human.

Law 7

Light Never Argues With Darkness

Light does not win by debating shadow. It wins by being what it is. You do not have to prove goodness to anything that feeds on reaction. Presence is stronger than performance. When you carry light, your calm becomes a boundary and your clarity becomes direction. Darkness fades because it cannot hold its shape without your attention.

Think of walking into a room at night. You do not speak to the dark. You reach for a switch. That is this law. When someone is baiting you, the switch is your steady breath. When a message is designed to provoke you, the switch is a quiet line that names the truth and ends the moment. The less you argue, the more you conserve power for what matters.

Arguing with darkness teaches it how to find you. It learns your buttons. It learns your schedule. It learns to grow strong on your time. Refusing the argument is not weakness. It is strategy. You move from reaction to authorship. You decide when and where your energy is used.

At home this shows up in small moments. A child speaks sharply. A partner comes in hot from a hard day. Your old habit might be to match volume or to deliver a long lesson in the heat of the moment. Light chooses a slower route. Name what is true in one line. I want respect in this room. Then set a simple next step. We will talk after we breathe and wash our hands. When calm returns, teach the skill that prevents the repeat. You did not argue. You reset the tone.

At work you will sometimes meet people who thrive on noise. They interrupt. They undermine. They send performative emails. Light does not join that play. Light documents facts and sets expectations. Thank you for the note. Here are the decisions and the owners. I will follow up Thursday. If the behavior continues, light escalates through correct channels without drama. You keep dignity and you keep receipts. Darkness loses air because you did not give it a show.

Online the rule is even more useful. Many posts are invitations to fight. Arguing feeds the loop. Light adds value once and leaves. Share the clear resource. Correct the harm with a source if safety allows. Then mute, block, or exit. Your peace is more important than winning people who came to watch rather than to learn.

This law needs your body to participate. Darkness pulls for speed. It wants the quick clap back. Train a reflex that slows you for three breaths. In through your nose. Hold for a count of two. Out through your mouth for six. Put your tongue on the roof of your mouth while you exhale. This quiets the jaw and the heartbeat. Now your face softens and your voice drops. You become the person in the room who is not available for chaos.

Light tells the truth. It simply refuses to fight with it. You can say no without a speech. You can set a boundary without a scene. I am not available for this tone. I can talk at two when we can be respectful. If the tone returns, end the call kindly and keep your promise to try again later. Do this twice. If respect does not appear, withdraw access. You did not argue. You protected dignity, including your own.

There will be moments when silence looks like surrender. This is where clarity helps. Add one clean sentence that names your aim. I care about a real solution. I will respond after I check the facts. That line tells an honest person why you are quiet. It also tells a dishonest person that you will not feed their game.

Light does not ignore harm. It chooses the action that reduces harm without adding heat. You can correct a falsehood with receipts. You can invite a third party into the conversation. You can move a thread from a crowd to a smaller room. You can put agreements in writing. These moves pour light on the path ahead. They do not pour energy into the fire.

When the darkness is inside you, the same rule applies. Do not argue with your own fear. Acknowledge it. Then turn on a switch. Drink water. Step outside. Put both feet on the ground and name five true things in the room. I am safe. The door is closed. The table is smooth. There is light in the window. I can choose my next step. You return to yourself. From there you act.

Keep language close that fits this law. Here is what is true. Here is what I will do. Here is when I will respond. I am stepping away now. These lines are short and kind. They move the moment forward without giving chaos a chance to multiply.

If you work in a role that faces the public, build structures that support this habit. Create a policy for rude messages so staff do not have to decide each time. Teach the script that names limits and offers the next right channel. Track patterns and set automatic filters. Light is not random. It is a system that protects peace.

Close with a simple practice. Pick one place where arguments steal your energy. The inbox. The family chat. The comment section. Write a two sentence response you will use for the next month. Sentence one names the value. I want clarity and respect. Sentence two sets the action. Here is the plan and timeline. If the other person keeps reaching for a fight, you repeat the response once and then you exit. You will find that results improve when performance disappears.

Light never argues with darkness. It does not chase. It does not beg. It chooses presence, truth, and boundaries. It keeps the house warm without feeding a fire. Carry that light. Let it guide your timing and your tone. Watch how the room changes when you stop wrestling shadows and start turning on switches.

Law 8

Truth Without Kindness Is Violence

Truth is a tool. It can mend or it can cut. The same sentence that heals a situation when spoken with care can damage a person when thrown like a stone. Kindness is the handle that makes truth safe to hold. When you pair truth with kindness, you keep dignity intact while you move things forward.

Many people use truth as permission to unload. They point to honesty and forget the impact of delivery. A raw fact shouted in a kitchen is not the same as a clear fact offered at a calm table. The difference is intention and tone. Ask yourself before you speak. Do I want to help this person grow or do I want to score a point. If the point is the aim, wait. If growth is the aim, shape the truth so it lands and stays.

Kindness does not hide reality. It wraps reality in respect. That respect changes how a nervous system receives hard news. The listener can hear the message without bracing against attack. This is how change becomes possible. People can learn when they do not feel like they must defend their worth.

At home, practice the order that keeps love steady. First, safety. Then, truth. A child breaks a rule and hopes you will not notice. You can correct without shaming. State what happened in plain words. This is the rule. Here is the part that broke. Then add the teaching and the repair. Here is how we will fix it now. Here is how we will try again tomorrow. The tone is firm and warm. The child learns and the relationship stays open.

With a partner, truth is most useful when it speaks about impact rather than character. You always and you never shut a door. Try this instead. When you cancel late, I feel small and unimportant. I would like a message earlier and a new time on the same day. Now the truth describes the effect and the need. It leaves room for a better choice next time.

At work, kindness helps truth do its job. A review that humiliates a person will produce fear, not quality. A review that names what missed, shows an example, and offers a path to improve builds skill. Say exactly what was off and why. Show one better model. Ask what help would make the next version stronger. People rise under that kind of truth because it treats them like adults who can learn.

Delivery matters. Volume, pacing, and face all send signals. Lower your voice when the topic is heavy. Slow your tempo so the words can be received. Keep your expression steady and open. This tells the other person that you are not a threat. You are a partner in repair. If emotions are high, separate the person from the behavior in your language. You are valuable here. This behavior is not working. That sentence keeps worth intact while you set a clear limit.

Timing matters too. Truth spoken in the heat of a flare will ride the heat. Wait for a window where the body can listen. That may be after water and a short walk. It may be the next morning when sleep has cooled the story in your head. A true sentence at the wrong time can cause harm. The same sentence at the right time can save a week.

Kindness also requires boundaries. If someone uses the language of honesty to justify cruelty, call it what it is. You are speaking in a way that does not respect me. I am open to feedback that comes with care. If the person refuses, step away. You are allowed to guard your spirit. You are not required to receive truth that arrives as a weapon.

There is a simple structure that keeps truth clean. Start with care. I want this to work for both of us. Name the fact. Here is what happened. Name the impact. Here is how it lands on me or on the team. Name the need. Here is what I am asking for next time. Invite response. What do you need from me. This short path creates clarity without injury.

Practice this structure in small places so it becomes natural. Use it in a text when a friend is late. Use it in a note when you give feedback on a draft. Use it with yourself when you miss a goal. Speak with care to your own heart. I missed the mark this week. The impact is stress and delay. I will plan my mornings tonight and protect two hours tomorrow. Truth gentled by kindness keeps motivation alive.

There will be moments when truth must be firm. Someone keeps crossing a line or a pattern of harm appears. Kindness in these moments looks like direct language and clear consequence, delivered without venom. I will not continue if this behavior repeats. If it does, I will step away from the project. Then follow through. The calm follow through is the kindest part. It teaches with consistency rather than with noise.

If you are not sure whether your truth carries kindness, check the results. After you speak, does the room soften. Do shoulders drop. Do you and the other person move toward a plan. If yes, your delivery worked. If not, adjust next time. Lower the volume. Use fewer words. Replace labels with descriptions. Change the place so it feels neutral. Truth gets better when you treat it as a craft.

Finish with a simple ritual. Before any hard conversation, write one line that sets your aim. My aim is clarity with care. Then choose one act that proves it. Pour water. Sit next to the person rather than across. Use a steady tone. When the talk is done, send a short summary that names the agreement. This protects both sides and prevents confusion.

Truth without kindness is violence. It bruises what it was meant to build. Truth with kindness is power that heals as it corrects. Carry both. Let your honesty be precise and your tone be humane. You will become a person whose words people can trust, even when those words are hard to hear.

Law 9

The Ego Hates Gentle Power

Ego prefers noise. It wants the room to notice, to react, to choose sides. Gentle power does the opposite. It settles the air. It lowers the flame. It does not need to perform, and that is why ego resents it. When you move with quiet confidence, people cannot grab you by volume or vanity. You become hard to provoke and easy to trust.

Gentle power is not the same as being small. It is grounded. It knows what it is protecting. It knows when to speak and when to pause. It leaves space for other people without giving up the center of its own values. The ego reads that calm as a threat because it cannot control it. It tries to bait you into proving yourself. You do not need to take the bait.

At home, ego often shows up as the need to be right in the moment. You can feel it rise when a partner remembers a detail differently or a child questions a rule. Gentle power chooses the relationship over the point. It says let us write the facts and choose a plan. It says I want respect here and I also want to understand what you felt. The result is progress without a winner and a loser.

At work, ego likes the stage. It pushes for the clever line in a meeting or the long email that shows you know more than everyone else. Gentle power keeps the task in front. It asks the clean question that gets to the heart of the problem. It credits the person who supplied the key insight. It moves a decision to a smaller room if the big room is turning performative. People come to rely on you because you spend your energy on outcomes rather than image.

Ego also disguises itself as urgency. It will tell you that speed proves leadership. Gentle power respects timing. It understands that a short pause can prevent a long repair. It holds a standard without making everything an emergency. When you practice this, teams learn to match your steadiness. Home learns it too.

Your body will tell you when ego is trying to drive. Jaw tight. Shoulders up. Heat in the chest. The words in your head sound like You will not talk to me like that or I have to make this land right now. When you notice those signals, return to center. Put your feet flat. Drop your shoulders one inch. Inhale for four counts, hold for two, exhale for six. This resets the nervous system so you can choose gentle power on purpose.

Language helps. Ego reaches for labels. You never. You always. Gentle power speaks in facts and needs. Here is what happened. Here is how it landed. Here is what I need next time. It also offers a path. Here is what I can do on my side. This way of talking keeps worth intact while it sets direction. People lean toward cooperation when they do not feel attacked.

Boundaries are essential. Gentle power is not agreeable to harm. It can say no without heat. It can end a call that is not respectful. It can move a conversation to a calmer time. A simple sentence works. I want a good outcome, and I am not available for this tone. I will return at three. Follow through quietly. The ego will want to add a speech. Do not feed it.

When others try to provoke you, remember that bait needs attention to work. A snide comment in a meeting. A message designed to sting. A story told to get a rise out of you. Gentle power refuses the show. It names the work, sets the next step, and moves on. If a pattern continues, it documents and escalates through proper channels. Calm process is harder to fight than a loud reply.

There is a test you can use to check whether ego or gentle power is steering. Ask yourself what am I trying to protect. If the answer is image, the ego is at the wheel. If the answer is the relationship, the standard, or the outcome, gentle power is in charge. Choose the second answer and let your tone match it.

Practice small. Choose one recurring moment where ego appears. The family group chat. A weekly sync. A pickup line at school. Decide in advance how gentle power will look there. One warm greeting. One clarifying question. One sentence that sets a limit if needed. Then repeat that move each time. Patterns beat impulse.

LAW 9

Give yourself gentleness too. Ego hates learning because learning includes moments of not knowing. Gentle power welcomes learning. It says I missed that. Thank you for catching it. I will fix it and send an update by noon. This kind of humility does not lower you. It raises trust. People believe you because you tell the truth about your role in the mess and your plan to repair it.

Protect your quiet windows. Gentle power grows in spaces where you are not constantly pulled. Guard an hour where no one can reach you. Walk without your phone. Sit in a chair and breathe before the day starts. The ego loses grip when you are not feeding it with comparison or noise. Your decisions come out cleaner.

If someone mistakes your calm for weakness, you can correct the read without changing your pace. Try a single line with eye contact. I care about results and respect. I am choosing careful words so we get both. Then return to the plan. They will learn what your calm means by the way you follow through.

Close with a simple ritual for the next seven days. Before a conversation that matters, write two lines in your notes. My intention is clarity with care. My boundary is dignity for all involved. Read them once out loud. Let your shoulders settle. Then go in and act like the person who wrote those lines. Watch what happens to the temperature of the room. Watch what happens to the results.

The ego hates gentle power because gentle power does not feed it. Gentle power does not need applause to prove it is strong.

It serves truth, timing, and respect. It keeps the house warm and the work moving. Choose it, and you will carry a presence that steadies the people around you and keeps your own peace intact.

Law 10

Patience Is the Highest Discipline

Patience is not passive. It is training. It is the choice to hold your energy steady while the right conditions form. You are not doing nothing. You are protecting quality. You are protecting dignity. You are protecting your peace so you can see the next honest step.

Think of a seed in dark soil. You do not dig it up every hour to check on it. You water it. You give it light. You keep the ground loose. You trust what you cannot see yet. That is the work of patience. You place your effort where it matters and you release the rest.

Impatience is loud. It says push harder right now. It judges every delay as failure. Patience is clear. It asks what action is useful and what action is noise. It keeps you from paying a high price for speed that will not last. It lets you move with care so results can hold their shape under pressure.

At home patience shows up in small habits. A child is learning how to tie shoes and the morning clock is ticking. You can take over and move fast. Or you can slow your voice, sit at their level, and coach the steps again. The second choice takes longer today and saves you weeks later. The child learns. You build trust. The house breathes.

With a partner patience keeps love from turning into scorekeeping. It sounds like I want to understand your view. It looks like listening until you can repeat their point without a twist. It feels like taking a short walk and returning to finish the talk when both bodies are calm. You are not avoiding the issue. You are creating conditions where truth can land without injury.

At work patience protects judgment. Most problems look simple at first and then widen. Give yourself time to collect the real facts. Write them on one page. What is known. What is assumed. Who is affected. What happens if we are wrong. Ask one more person whose view will be shaped by the decision. This is not delay for the sake of delay. This is discipline. Your team learns to trust your calls because they are made from a full picture.

Patience is also how you become skillful. You will not master a craft by rushing from one trick to the next. Choose one slice of the work and practice it with intention. Ten quiet minutes every day beat three frantic hours once a month. Keep a short log. Note what improved. Note what still needs attention. The log will keep you honest on days when your feelings do not match your progress.

Your body can help you practice this law. When impatience

rises, your jaw tightens and your breath gets shallow. Teach your body a short reset you can use anywhere. Inhale through your nose for four counts. Hold for two. Exhale for six. Lower your shoulders one inch. Keep your eyes soft. When your body settles, your words will become kinder and your choices cleaner.

Patience does not mean you accept harm. It means you choose timing that protects dignity while you set limits. You can say I will not continue this conversation while voices are raised. I will return at two. You can say I am not ready to decide this today. I will send my answer tomorrow at noon. You are not letting the moment drift. You are anchoring it to a clear time and a clear action.

There will be people who try to use your patience as a place to hide. That is not what this law asks of you. If promises keep slipping, move from patience to process. Put agreements in writing. Add checkpoints. Shorten timelines. Decide what happens if a step is missed. Calm structure is a form of kindness. It removes confusion and it protects the work.

Patience with yourself matters as much as patience with others. You are learning in real time. You will make a choice you regret. You will take longer than you planned. Speak to yourself in clean sentences. I missed the mark. Here is what I will try next. Here is when I will check again. That tone keeps you moving. Shame freezes progress. Simple honesty keeps it alive.

Language can support this practice. Keep a few lines nearby. I am thinking. Give me a moment. I want to get this right, not just fast. Let us put the facts on one page. I will send a clear plan by morning. These sentences slow the spin without stopping momentum. They teach others that your pace serves quality, not ego.

Use small anchors to build the habit. A cup of water before you speak. One written summary at the end of a meeting. A rule that you do not send the first draft of a heated message. A quiet walk around the block before a high stakes call. Each anchor makes patience visible. People adjust to what you model.

Check your results. After you choose patience, does the room feel calmer. Do decisions hold. Do you sleep better. If yes, keep going. If not, adjust the measure. Add a deadline. Ask for help sooner. Remove steps that only look productive. Patience improves with use. It becomes precise.

Try this short practice tonight. Write one sentence that names the thing you want to rush. Next to it, write the smallest useful step you can take in the next hour. Do that step and stop. Tomorrow, take the next one. You will notice that steady steps beat frantic sprints. You will notice that people respond better to a calm rhythm.

Patience is the highest discipline because it protects every other skill. It guards your tone, your timing, your plan, and your relationships. It turns scattered effort into a clear path. Hold it like a craft. Practice it in your home, your work, and your own thoughts. The pace may look simple from the outside. The results will speak for themselves.

Law 11

Kindness Requires Boundaries

Kindness is not endless access. It is care with shape. Without shape, kindness turns into exhaustion and quiet resentment. With shape, kindness becomes a steady light that does not burn you up. A boundary is simply the line that protects what lets you be kind in the first place. Your sleep. Your time. Your safety. Your attention.

Think about a garden. Fences do not make it less beautiful. They keep out what would trample it and protect what is growing. Your life works the same way. When you name your lines and keep them, your kindness stays clean. You can show up fully where you intend to show up. You do not give from fumes and then feel angry about it later.

Boundaries begin with honesty. Before you say yes, ask one quiet question. Do I have the time, energy, and willingness to do this well. If the answer is no, the kind choice is a clear no. If the answer is yes, the kind choice is a clear yes with edges. I can do this by Friday. I can help for one hour. I can talk after dinner, not right now. Edges protect both sides from confusion and disappointment.

At home, boundaries sound like calm rules that keep love steady. Speak to me with respect. Knock before you enter my room. Screens off at dinner. These are not punishments. They are structures that make the house gentle to live in. When a rule is crossed, respond with repair, not rage. This is the line. Here is what happens next. We will try again tomorrow. Children learn faster when the lines are simple and predictable.

With a partner, boundaries allow closeness to be safe. Say what you need plainly. I want direct communication. I do not want threats to leave during conflict. If something hard must be said, choose timing that protects both of us. If a pattern hurts you, say so early. I feel small when plans change last minute. I need a text as soon as you know and a new time on the same day. You are not trying to control another person. You are sharing what keeps the relationship fit for your heart.

At work, kindness without boundaries turns into a workload that grows without limit. Protect your focus. Put deep work time on your calendar. Use a short template for requests so people give you what you need the first time. What is the goal. What is due. Who decides. When someone pushes past your limits, stay steady and specific. I can deliver this part by Wednesday. I cannot take the extra scope without moving the date. Clear and calm language saves the project and your health.

Boundaries are also for your body. A soft voice and warm eye contact do not require that you stay in a room that feels unsafe. You can step out. You can say I am not comfortable. I am leaving now. You can choose a different seat. You can turn a video call into audio. Your nervous system is part of this law. When it settles, your kindness becomes possible again.

Some people will test your lines. They will act hurt when you say no or try to debate your limit. Stay gentle and repeat yourself once. Then end the loop. I understand this is disappointing. My answer is still no. I wish you well. If the testing continues, reduce contact or add structure. Communicate by email. Keep agreements in writing. Limit access to set hours. You are not cruel. You are wise about what the relationship can hold.

Language is your friend here. Keep a few ready lines that sound like you. I cannot do that, and I hope you find what you need. I am available from two to four. I can help with A or B, not both. I appreciate the invitation, and I am going to pass. Thank you for understanding. These sentences are doors that close softly. They keep the air warm while they protect your time.

Remember that boundaries are not just for saying no. They help you say a clean yes. When you accept a request, set the terms as part of the gift. I can lead the meeting if we keep it to thirty minutes and use an agenda. I will host on Sunday if we keep it simple. I will review the draft if I have 24 hours. Now your yes has a container. It is much easier to deliver with grace.

Self respect is the root of this law. When you keep your word to yourself, others learn how to treat you. If you decide to end a call when voices rise, follow through. If you choose no phone in the bedroom, honor it even when the scroll is tempting. Quiet consistency teaches faster than any speech. Over time, the people around you adjust to your lines because your lines do not move.

There will be guilt at first. That is normal. Most of us were trained to measure kindness by how much we give up. Try a small reset. Measure kindness by how much dignity remains after you act, yours included. If your yes erases your peace, it was not a kind yes. If your no protects the relationship from resentment, it was a kind no.

Check results to calibrate. After you hold a boundary, do you feel lighter. Do conversations get clearer. Do you have more patience where you meant to spend it. If yes, you are on the right path. If not, adjust the line. Sometimes it needs to be firmer. Sometimes it needs to be explained in writing. Sometimes it needs a consequence that is real and calm.

End with a practice for the week. Choose one room of your life that feels crowded. Write one boundary for that room. One sentence only. Read it aloud in a steady voice. Tell the person who needs to know. Then keep it for seven days. Notice what happens to your energy, your tone, and your sleep.

Kindness requires boundaries because kindness needs a healthy place to live. Your lines protect that place. They turn your care into something durable. They make your yes trustworthy and your no clean. Hold your lines with a warm heart and a steady hand. You will have more to give and a life that feels like yours.

Law 12

Your Energy Teaches Before You Speak

People feel you before they hear you. The room reads your posture, your eyes, your breath, and the way you enter a space. That reading happens in seconds. If your energy is hurried, others brace. If your energy is settled, others open. Before a single word, you have already taught everyone what to expect from you.

Think of stepping into a lobby two minutes before a meeting. If you arrive with shallow breath and a clipped pace, nearby shoulders rise. If you arrive with an easy step, steady eyes, and one calm greeting, the group settles. The same is true on a call or in a text thread. Your energy sets the first lesson. Choose it on purpose.

Your body carries messages long before your mouth does. Shoulders up and jaw tight say hurry and defend. Shoulders down and eyes warm say we are safe to think. When you want kindness to lead, train simple signals. Put both feet flat on the floor. Unclench your jaw. Let your breath drop into your belly. Lift your chest one inch. These cues cost nothing and change everything.

Now add the power of respectful address. Your line is true and practical: "Saying yes sir or yes mamn can completely change how a person views you." Courtesy phrases act like switches. They signal humility, presence, and care in a single beat. They tell another nervous system that you are here to cooperate, not to compete. Use what fits the person and the setting. Yes sir. Yes ma'am. Yes, Coach. Yes, Officer. Often the person's name is best. Yes, Ms. Rivera. Thank you, Malik. Respect in your words changes how your energy is received.

This is not about shrinking yourself. It is about opening the channel so truth can travel. Respectful address works because it lowers threat. People who feel respected listen longer and think clearer. You still hold boundaries. You still tell the truth. You simply wrap the truth in a tone that keeps dignity intact on both sides.

At home, your energy can make ordinary moments gentle. Before you call a child to do a task, take one slow inhale and one longer exhale. Walk to them instead of shouting across rooms. Kneel or sit so your eyes are level. Say the request in one sentence and add a small courtesy. Yes, buddy, it is time to put shoes on. Thank you for moving quickly. The job gets done faster because your energy did not turn a small thing into a fight.

With a partner, energy is often the whole message. If you begin a hard talk with tension, the other person goes on guard. Start with presence. Place a hand on the table. Look at them fully. Use a warm opener. I want us to do well here. Then speak your truth. Respect words help here too. Thank you for listening. Yes, I hear your view. Here is my need. The honesty lands because your tone already said I am for us.

At work, your energy writes the tone of the day. Arrive two minutes early and settle your breath before the meeting starts. Greet people by name. Sit with a posture that is upright and at ease. When you need focus, lower your voice rather than raising it. When you need urgency, be clear about time and next steps instead of pouring pressure into the room. People follow energy that feels steady and useful.

Your energy travels through writing. A message sent in a rush can sound sharp even if the words are polite. Read your notes out loud before you hit send. If you hear tension, change the order. Begin with the aim, state the fact, name the need, close with thanks. Add one warm line if the topic is heavy. Thank you for the effort here. That single sentence lowers shoulders on the other side of the screen.

Intention shapes energy. Before a conversation, name your aim in one sentence. My aim is clarity with care. Let that sentence guide your tone, your volume, and your timing. If you feel yourself sliding into performance or defense, pause and repeat the aim in your head. Your body will adjust. Your words will follow.

Repair is part of teaching too. When you walk in hot and see the room change, do not push through it. Own it in one sentence. I came in tense. Let me reset. Take a breath, soften your face, and begin again. People learn more from your repair than from a speech about calm. They see what leadership looks like in real life.

Boundaries support clean energy. You will teach better when you are not stretched to the edge. Protect sleep. Keep small quiet windows with no chatter and no screens. Say no early when you cannot give your best. A tired body teaches hurry and impatience. A cared for body teaches steadiness without a word.

Keep phrases that pair respect with clarity. Yes, sir, I will send the summary by noon. Yes, ma'am, I can help for thirty minutes. Thank you for raising that point. Here is what I can do today. If sir or ma'am does not fit the culture you are in, use the person's name or title. The principle is the same. Lead with respect so your message has a safe place to land.

Notice the spaces that change your energy and choose wisely. Some rooms raise your blood pressure before you sit down. Some rooms help you breathe. When you can, have important talks in spaces that keep you grounded. If you must be in a hard place, arrive early and set yourself. Water. Breath. Posture. Aim. You can bring the gentle space with you.

Teach children and teams how to do this by letting them see you practice. Say out loud what you are doing. I am taking one breath so I can listen better. I am going to slow my voice so we can think. I am saying yes, Coach, so we both know I heard the instruction. People around you pick up the habit because you made it visible and simple.

End with a one minute routine. Step one, put both feet flat. Step two, inhale for four, hold for two, exhale for six. Step three, soften your eyes and lift your chest one inch. Step four, choose a respectful opener that fits the person. Yes, ma'am. Yes, Mr. Lee. Thank you for your time. Step five, name your aim in one sentence. Then speak. Try this before a call, before a correction, before you walk in the door at night. You will feel the difference and so will everyone else.

Your energy teaches before you speak. Let it teach safety, respect, and direction. Choose presence over hurry. Choose courtesy over noise. Choose a tone that keeps dignity intact. When your energy comes first and your respect is audible, the room understands you before the first sentence lands.

Law 13

Compassion Without Wisdom Is Self-Destruction

Compassion is a beautiful force, but it needs guidance. Without wisdom, compassion says yes when it should pause. It pours from an empty cup. It softens what should be strengthened. Over time that kind of giving turns you into someone you do not recognize. Your sleep goes. Your patience thins. Resentment grows in the place where love used to live. Wise compassion prevents that. It asks, Who am I helping, and how do I help without harming myself or the truth.

Compassion wants to relieve pain. Wisdom studies the pattern. If a request repeats with no change, wisdom steps in. It asks for ownership. It names the cost. It sets a boundary so the help becomes seed and not fertilizer for the same problem. This does not make you cold. It makes your care effective.

At home this can look simple. A teenager forgets the same task every week. Compassion says I know you are busy. Wisdom adds structure. Write the steps. Put the list where the work happens. Tie the privilege to the task. You can go out after the kitchen is clean. Now your care teaches skill and protects your peace.

With a partner, compassion listens. Wisdom asks the clean question. Do you want comfort or a plan. If comfort is the answer, you sit close and let the storm pass. If a plan is the answer, you move with clarity. Here is what I can do. Here is what I need from you. Both choices are loving. Both choices prevent you from carrying what is not yours.

In friendship, compassion often tries to rescue. Wisdom refuses to be the net for every fall. It offers presence and it offers a path. I can talk for twenty minutes tonight. I cannot be your only support. Here are two resources that can hold you longer. You stay kind and you stay honest about your limits. The friendship becomes healthier because the weight is shared.

At work, compassion sees a person under pressure. Wisdom protects the standard. You can say I see this is heavy. I will help you triage. Then you reduce scope, set checkpoints, and write decisions so the team does not drown again next week. You are not being hard. You are making sure that care for one person does not turn into harm for five others.

Your body will tell you when compassion is drifting into self-destruction. You feel a tightness in your chest when their name appears on your phone. You feel dread after you say yes. You hear yourself vent about the same situation in loops. Treat these signals like alarms. Pause before you answer. Ask the questions that return you to wisdom.

Here are four questions to keep close. One. What is my capacity today. Two. What outcome am I trying to create. Three. What is their part to carry. Four. What boundary will keep the relationship kind tomorrow. If you cannot answer, you are not ready to say yes. You can reply with care and clarity. I want to help and I need an hour to think. I will text you with what I can offer.

Wise compassion includes consequence. If someone breaks trust, the repair must fit the harm. That might mean a timeout for access, a written plan, or a change in role. Compassion without consequence breeds repeat injuries. Compassion with consequence creates learning. You can say I forgive you and I am changing how we work for the next month. The tone is warm. The line is firm.

Self compassion is part of this law. You cannot offer clean care if you treat yourself like a machine. Keep the simple practices that refill you. Sleep. Water. Movement. Quiet. Protect small windows where no one can reach you. Guard a hobby that has nothing to do with helping anyone. These choices are not selfish. They are maintenance for the person your people rely on.

Language helps you hold the line. Use steady sentences that honor both care and limits. I am not able to do that, and I hope you find what you need. I can help with this part by Friday. I am willing to listen, not to be spoken to in that tone. If this repeats, I will step back for a while. Speak them calmly. Then keep them. Your consistency will teach faster than any lecture.

There will be people who call your boundaries unkind. Remember the measure. Does this choice protect dignity, including mine. Does it move us toward truth and growth. If yes, keep the boundary. If no, adjust the shape. You are learning. Wisdom grows through trial, reflection, and correction. Offer yourself the same patience you offer others.

A short practice for the week. Pick one relationship that leaves you drained. Write three lines. What I have been doing. How it has affected me. What I will do instead. For example. I take every late call. I wake tired and short with my family. I will answer within daylight hours and send resources for the rest. Tell the person with a warm tone. Then follow your new plan for seven days. Watch how your energy changes. Often the other person adjusts once the pattern does.

Compassion without wisdom is self-destruction. Compassion with wisdom is durable love. It keeps your heart soft and your life intact. It helps people rise instead of keeping them dependent. It turns your yes into something that lasts. Choose it on purpose. Let your care be kind and let it be clear. That is how you stay generous for the long run.

Law 14

What You Resist, You Reinforce

Whatever you battle with your attention grows teeth. Anger fed with more anger hardens. Fear fed with more fear multiplies. When you keep pushing against a thing that will not move, your energy becomes the fuel that keeps it standing. Kindness moves differently. It names what is real, removes the extra noise, and directs effort where it will actually change the outcome.

This law is not asking you to ignore harm. It is asking you to stop feeding it. The first move is to see the loop. Notice where you grip. Notice the story that repeats. I will not let them win. I will make them understand. Your jaw tightens and your thoughts circle. That is the sign you are reinforcing the very problem you want to solve.

At home, resistance shows up as power struggles over small things. A child refuses a task and you raise your voice to match. The moment turns into a contest and the task is lost. Choose a different route. Lower your tone. Name the fact and the next step. The toys are on the floor. We are putting them in the bin together for five minutes. Set a timer. Offer one choice that keeps the goal intact. Now the room has direction instead of a tug of war.

With a partner, resistance turns repair into debate. You argue about who interrupted whom rather than about respect. Step out of the loop. Speak to the principle rather than the score. I want a conversation where both of us can finish a sentence. Let us try again at seven with that rule. You did not yield your value. You stopped reinforcing the fight and started building a structure that keeps both of you human.

At work, resistance often appears as a running battle with a person or a pattern. The undermining email. The meeting that always turns messy. The policy that blocks progress. Rather than venting in circles, pour energy into process. Move decisions into writing. Clarify owners and timelines. Invite a neutral third voice. If a behavior continues, escalate calmly through the channel that exists. The heat comes down and the signal goes up. You are no longer feeding the show.

Your body helps you keep this law. Resistance lives in muscles first. Shoulders up. Breath shallow. Hands tight. When you feel it, pause for a short reset. Inhale through your nose for four counts. Hold for two. Exhale for six. Drop your shoulders one inch. Look at something steady in the room. Ask one question. What action moves this forward. Then do that action within the hour.

Language is a tool here. Replace fighting words with directing words. Instead of You always do this try Here is what happened and here is what we need next time. Instead of I refuse to accept this try I am choosing this plan and this timeline. Instead of I will prove you wrong try I will document the facts and follow the process. You are not giving up. You are choosing the only lane that leads to change.

Online this law saves your peace. Many posts are invitations to resist. Arguing keeps the thread alive and teaches bad faith actors what to press. Add value once if it is safe. Link to a clear source. Then mute, block, or leave. Put your attention where it yields fruit. Your mind will thank you and your day will open.

This law also applies inside your own thoughts. The more you fight a fear, the louder it knocks. Do not argue with it. Acknowledge it and give it a job that is small. I hear you. You are trying to protect me. Your job is to remind me to prepare for the call. Now I am going to prepare. Then move. Open the document. Outline three points. Send one email. Action drains the power of the story.

Boundaries are not resistance. They are design. When a pattern harms you, set a clear line and keep it without drama. I do not take calls after nine. I will not continue if voices rise. I will respond by email so we have a record. Each line removes friction. Each line starves the loop of the attention it needs to continue.

There will be people who read your refusal to argue as weakness. Clarify once. I care about results and respect. I will work through the plan we agreed on. Then return to the plan. Follow

LAW 14

through quietly. Results teach faster than defense ever will.

Use a small weekly practice to strengthen this habit. Pick one situation that keeps stealing your attention. Write the loop you want to stop. Write the outcome you want instead. Write the smallest step that moves toward that outcome. Do the step. Review in two days. Adjust and repeat. Steady replacement beats steady resistance.

Kindness dissolves what argument keeps alive. It turns you from a reactor into an author. You are no longer pulled into every tug. You place your attention like a tool. You speak simply. You set a structure. You leave a room when it refuses respect. Over time the noise fades because you stopped feeding it.

What you resist, you reinforce. What you redirect, you reshape. Let your energy bow to intention, not to the hook. Choose the action that makes the future a little clearer. Choose the tone that keeps dignity intact. Choose the plan that can be checked on a page. When you spend your attention this way, the world around you begins to match your aim.

Law 15

Softness Is a Weapon

Softness is not weakness. It is precision. It is the choice to be fully present and fully human while you protect what matters. Hardness swings wide and wastes energy. Softness lands where it counts. It lowers defenses. It opens ears. It makes space for the truth to do its work.

Think of warm water on a stained cup. You could scrape and scratch. Or you can let steady warmth loosen what force cannot. Softness works the same way. Your tone lowers. Your face settles. Your words carry air around them. The person in front of you stops bracing and starts listening. Rooms change when you choose this temperature.

Softness begins inside the body. Before you speak, check your breath. Inhale through your nose for four counts. Hold for two. Exhale for six. Let your shoulders fall one inch. Put both feet flat. These small choices tell your nervous system that you are safe to think. Your voice will come out warm. Your eyes will be kind without losing clarity. People feel it before a single sentence lands.

At home, softness is power that teaches. A child spills the juice and goes stiff with fear. You could lecture and win the moment, yet lose the lesson. Or you can kneel, put a towel in their hand, and say, We will clean it together. After the floor is dry you can show a better way to carry the cup. The child learns skill and keeps dignity. Tomorrow is easier because today did not become a storm.

With a partner, softness protects closeness while you tell the truth. You can say, When plans change last minute I feel small, and I need a text as soon as you know. The words are clear. The tone is steady. You are not trying to score a point. You are naming what keeps the relationship kind. Softness makes repair possible because it invites a reply rather than a defense.

At work, softness is operational. It says, Here are the facts. Here is what missed. Here is what we will do next. It credits by name. It keeps voice and email clean of sarcasm. It moves tense topics into smaller rooms and uses a whiteboard to separate problem from person. When people are not busy protecting themselves, they will protect the goal. That is the quiet math of softness.

Softness carries boundaries. The myth says you must be sharp to be safe. The truth is simpler. You can say no in a gentle voice. You can end a meeting that has turned disrespectful with one plain line. I want a good outcome for both of us. I will return when we can speak with respect. Then follow through. The follow through is the sharp edge. The tone stays soft so the lesson stays teachable.

Language matters. Keep a few phrases that hold shape without heat. I want to understand. Here is what I can offer. Here is what I need. Let us write the plan and date. Thank you for the part you did. These lines carry authority wrapped in care. They move the group toward a decision. They also model how power can sound when it does not need to perform.

Softness is strategic when you face aggression. A raised voice pulls for more volume. Do not match it. Speak slower. Sit back an inch. Lower your chin a little so your face reads ease, not challenge. Name the value and the next step. We both want a solution. Here is the decision we need today. If the pattern repeats, take it to process rather than a fight. Document the facts. Invite a second set of eyes. Softness does not skip accountability. It refuses theater.

Online, softness keeps you sane. Many posts are written to harvest reaction. Add value once, then choose silence. Share a clear source. Correct the false point with one sentence if safety allows. Then mute or step away. Your peace is not a prize for strangers to win. It is a resource you steward on purpose.

Softness includes self talk. You cannot offer gentle power to others while you punish yourself. When you miss a mark, speak to yourself like you would speak to someone you love. I missed it. Here is why. Here is my next small step. This tone refuels effort. Shame drains it. Softness inside creates softness that is safe for others to meet.

There will be people who mistake softness for permission. Correct the read without changing your temperature. I care about results and respect. If this behavior continues I will step away. Then keep your word. Quiet consistency will teach what your tone might not. Over time even difficult people learn what your softness means. It means calm, not surrender. It means truth, not theater.

Softness is also design. Remove friction so kindness has room to live. Label the bin. Share the checklist. Put the decision in writing. Return what you borrowed better than you found it. Small gentle choices create a path that carries weight without noise. You save your strength for the places where it is truly needed.

Practice brings this law to life. Try a simple ritual for the next seven days. Before any tense moment, pause for one breath. Name your aim in a private sentence. My aim is clarity with care. Choose one soft behavior that proves it. Sit beside instead of across. Pour water. Lower your voice. When the talk ends, send a short summary with thanks and next steps. Watch how meetings end faster. Watch how homes feel lighter.

Test your results. After you choose softness, do shoulders drop. Do people tell more truth. Do you sleep better. If yes, increase the dose. If no, add a boundary. A soft voice works best with a firm plan. Adjust your mix until the room reflects your intention.

Softness is a weapon because it disarms fear. It opens the door for truth. It carries consequences without cruelty. It creates progress that holds. Use it in your words, in your posture, in your timing, and in your exits. People will feel safe near you. Work will move. Home will breathe. And your life will keep its glow even when the day is sharp.

Law 16

Pain Is the Price of Empathy

Real empathy costs something. You feel a fraction of what another person feels and you agree to hold some of the weight for a little while. That slight ache in the chest. That squeeze in the throat. The tiredness after a long talk. These are the receipts. Empathy is not free, and that is why it is precious. When you understand the price, you stop pretending it should be painless. You also learn how to pay wisely so you do not burn out.

Empathy begins with consent. You choose to open your senses to someone's world. You pause your own story long enough to let theirs in. That opening will bring a pinch. Do not treat the pinch as a problem. Treat it as a sign that you are present. Then decide how much you can carry today and for how long. Care is a gift. It needs a container.

At home, empathy sounds like patience where you used to deliver a lecture. A child melts down after a hard day. You kneel so your eyes meet. You breathe with them until the storm passes. Only then do you speak about homework or chores. The order matters. Presence first. Instruction second. The task gets done, and the relationship stays soft.

With a partner, empathy protects closeness. Before you offer a fix, ask the question that keeps your heart open. Do you want comfort or a plan. If they say comfort, you move near and listen. If they say plan, you help design next steps. You are still paying a price to feel what they feel. You are paying it with purpose rather than with unhelpful worry.

At work, empathy is a performance advantage when it is paired with clarity. You notice who looks overwhelmed before deadlines slip. You name it gently and adjust scope or sequence. You write decisions so the team can stop guessing. You do not take on everyone's feelings. You create conditions that make the work humane. This is generous and it is efficient.

Your body will tell you when empathy is turning into overload. There is a dull headache after every call. You sigh before opening your messages. You feel dread when a certain name appears. Treat these signals as useful data. They do not mean you are unkind. They mean your container needs a stronger shape.

Give your empathy edges so it can last. Edges can be time, topic, or channel. I can talk for twenty minutes tonight. We will focus on what helps this week. Let us move this to text so I can think and send resources. Edges do not make you cold. They make you reliable. People will learn that your yes means full presence within limits that protect both of you.

Empathy asks for recovery. Build small rituals that clear the residue. Drink water. Step into sunlight for five minutes. Write three lines about what you heard and one line about what you will do, then close the notebook. Wash your hands and name what is true in the room. My floor is solid. The window is bright. I am safe. These simple practices tell your nervous system to return home.

There is a difference between empathy and merging. Empathy says I am with you. Merging says I am you. Empathy keeps your feet on your own ground. That is the only way you can help. Merging removes the air from the room. You lose view of choices and both of you go under. When you feel yourself sliding into the other person's feeling as if it were your own, pull back to breath and posture. Sit tall. Place both feet flat. Let what you heard pass through you rather than stick to you.

Language keeps empathy clean. Try lines like these. I hear the weight of this. Here is what I can offer today. Here is one next step that would lighten the load. If someone is speaking to you in a way that hurts, say I want to help. I need us to speak with respect so I can stay present. If a pattern repeats with no change, shift to boundaries and resources. I am not able to keep doing late night calls. Here are two numbers and an office hour I can keep.

Some people will try to use your heart as a permanent solution. That is not empathy. That is erosion. You can love someone and still refuse to be their only bridge. Invite more supports. Move heavy conversations to daylight. Put promises in writing so progress can be seen. Calm structure protects the bond and your well being.

Self empathy matters. Speak to yourself the way you speak to someone you would never abandon. You are tired because you care. Rest now. You did what you could today. Try again tomorrow with a smaller step. That tone keeps your heart soft. It prevents the bitterness that comes when you expect yourself to carry every weight without a break.

There will be moments when empathy asks for a larger price. You will sit with someone who is grieving. You will show up at the hospital. You will drive across town and say nothing except I am here. In those moments you are spending real energy. Honor the spend. Do less elsewhere for a while. Let the house be simple. Ask for help. Empathy is a communal practice. You are allowed to be part of the circle rather than the whole circle.

End with a one minute check you can use every day. Ask three questions. What pain near me needs presence. What is my capacity right now. What simple act offers relief without breaking me. Then do that act and stop. Send the text. Carry a bag to a car. Make a pot of soup and leave it on a porch. You will feel the small ache that proves you showed up. You will also feel the quiet pride that says you paid the price wisely.

Pain is the price of empathy. Pay it with intention. Give from a full heart with clear edges. Recover what you spend. In doing so you become a person who can sit with real life without hardening against it. That is strength. That is kindness with roots.

Law 17

Forgiveness Is Self-Defense

Forgiveness is not a gift to the person who harmed you. It is a release valve for your own nervous system. Anger that stays too long becomes a habit. It steals your sleep, crowds your thoughts, and turns the body into a place of constant alarms. Forgiveness cuts the cord between you and the injury so you can heal and protect yourself with a clear mind.

Forgiveness is not forgetting. It is not pretending nothing happened. It does not erase consequence. Forgiveness says I will not carry your choice inside my chest any longer. It returns the weight to its owner and frees your hands to build a life that is not shaped by that moment.

Forgiveness and reconciliation are different tasks. Forgiveness can be yours alone. Reconciliation requires safety and proof that repair is possible. You can forgive and still keep distance. You can forgive and still end a relationship. You can forgive and still ask for repayment or a plan that prevents the harm from repeating. This clarity keeps forgiveness strong rather than sentimental.

At home, forgiveness keeps love from hardening. A partner forgets an important promise. A child speaks out of turn and hurts your feelings. If you hold the sting, the room grows tense and your tone turns cold. Speak early and simple. Here is what happened. Here is how it landed. Here is what I need next time. Once the plan is set, forgive on purpose. Release the replay in your mind. Do not use the mistake as a future weapon. Trust grows because you chose repair over scorekeeping.

In friendship, forgiveness keeps you from living as a judge. People miss cues. People are late. People go quiet when life is heavy. Offer a clean path back when the person is worth keeping. I felt let down. I care about this friendship. Can we reset and name a way that works for both of us. If the pattern continues, choose distance without bitterness. You can keep your heart soft while you keep your time protected.

At work, forgiveness is a performance skill. Teams move faster when people correct and continue rather than linger in blame. You can say I was frustrated yesterday. I have let it go. Here is the plan to finish well. You are not ignoring the miss. You are preventing resentment from becoming the culture.

Your body knows when forgiveness is due. The story plays in your head at night. Your jaw clenches when their name appears. Your shoulders rise when the topic comes up. Treat these signals like a check engine light. Sit with your feet flat. Breathe in for four counts and out for six. Name the truth out loud. I was hurt. It mattered. I am ready to stop carrying this pain as my identity. Then choose an action that proves it. Write the boundary. Return the keys. Send the one sentence that closes the loop. Or choose silence and move on.

Forgiveness becomes safer when it has edges. You can forgive and still ask for accountability. You can forgive and still choose new rules for access. You can forgive and still prefer not to see certain people at certain events. When you design the edges, forgiveness becomes a shield rather than an open door.

Language helps. Keep a few lines ready so your heart and mouth agree. I forgive you. I am not reopening the past. I accept the apology and I need time before we are close again. I wish you well and I am stepping away. These sentences are short and kind. They keep dignity intact while they protect your peace.

There will be injuries that feel too large to forgive today. Honor that truth without turning it into a permanent sentence. You can say I am not ready to forgive and I am committed to healing. You can forgive in layers. First for the lost time. Later for the lost trust. Later still for the way you treated yourself while you were hurting. Each layer frees more room in your life.

Forgiveness is a choice you may need to repeat. Old memories rise. New details surface. When they do, return to the practice. Breathe. Name the truth. Choose the boundary. Release the hook again. Repetition is not failure. It is how the body learns that it is safe to let go.

If you worry that forgiveness makes you vulnerable, look at

results. After a true act of forgiveness, do you think more clearly. Do you sleep better. Do your decisions come out cleaner. That is self defense. You become less reactive. You choose from values rather than from injury. You stop losing hours to rehearsing speeches in your head. Your life moves forward because your attention is finally free.

Children learn this law from what you model. Let them see you apologize. Let them see you forgive. Let them hear you say I am choosing peace and here is the boundary that keeps us honest. They will grow up believing that strength and softness can share a room.

Try a short practice to close this chapter. Write the name of the person or event that still hooks you. Write three sentences. What happened. What boundary protects me now. What I am releasing. Say the sentences out loud in a calm voice. Tear the page or place it in a drawer. Then take one visible step that aligns with the boundary. Block a number. Decline an invite. Set a new rule for yourself and keep it for the next thirty days.

Forgiveness is self defense because it disarms what would keep living inside you. It returns your breath. It clears your judgment. It opens your hands so you can hold the present with strength. Choose it on purpose. Guard it with boundaries. Let it be the quiet practice that keeps your spirit light while your life stays grounded and real.

Law 18

Peace Speaks Louder Than Revenge

Revenge looks powerful for a moment. It gives a quick spark and then leaves a room full of smoke. Peace looks quiet at first. It clears the air so everyone can see what is true. Peace is not the same as being passive. Peace is decisive. It protects dignity. It chooses actions that end the cycle instead of feeding it. That is why peace speaks louder. It lasts.

Revenge is a mirror. You end up reflecting the very harm you wanted to correct. Peace is a window. It lets light in so the right next step becomes visible. When you choose peace, you are not excusing what happened. You are refusing to let it write your character. You are choosing a path that leaves you proud when the noise is over.

At home this law shows up in the small scenes. A child lies and you feel the sting. Revenge would be a sharp lecture that gives you relief and teaches fear. Peace looks like calm truth and repair. State what happened. State the impact. Then set a consequence that teaches skill. You will call the neighbor and return the item. We will practice how to ask next time. The house stays steady and the lesson holds.

With a partner, revenge shows up as cold tone, subtle jabs, or keeping score. The cost is closeness. Peace sounds like I was hurt by what happened yesterday. I want respect and I also want us to work. Here is what I need next time. Here is what I can offer on my side. You protect your worth without shrinking theirs. The relationship gets a chance to grow instead of calcifying around a wound.

At work, revenge hides in emails. It is the extra sentence that embarrasses a colleague or the cc meant to shame rather than inform. Those choices feel strong for an hour and then weaken the culture for months. Peace writes clean notes. Here are the facts. Here is what missed. Here is the plan and owners. If a pattern continues, peace uses process. Document, escalate to the right channel, and keep your voice even. You are not letting it slide. You are choosing the route that fixes the issue and protects the team.

Peace needs your body to help. Revenge burns hot. It speeds your breath and tightens your jaw. When you notice that heat, slow yourself for one minute. Inhale through your nose for four counts. Hold for two. Exhale for six. Drop your shoulders. Put both feet flat. Ask three questions. What is the truth. What protects dignity. What action moves this forward. Then do that action within the day.

Peace is not silence in the face of harm. It is a way of speaking that carries weight without poison. Use language that separates the person from the behavior and that names a specific change. I value our work and I cannot accept this approach. Here is the standard. Here is what happens if it repeats. When you follow through calmly you teach more than any clever insult could teach.

Some people will try to interpret peace as weakness. Correct the read once with a clear sentence. I care about results and respect. I am choosing process over performance. Then return to the plan. Keep receipts. Meet your own deadlines. Over time the room learns what your calm means. It means you are serious enough to trade a quick win for a durable one.

Peace also protects your private life. Revenge lingers. It keeps you up at night writing speeches in your head. Peace lets you sleep. You may still feel sadness or anger, but you are not feeding those feelings with extra stories. You gave the moment the right container. You let the rest pass through. Your mornings belong to your future again.

Online this law will save your attention. Many posts are designed to harvest outrage. Reply once with a clear source if it is safe. Then mute, block, or exit. Your purpose is not to be the internet's referee. Your purpose is to be a builder. Put your energy where it can plant something.

Boundaries make peace possible. If a person continues to cross lines, reduce access. Move conversations into writing. Bring a neutral party. Shorten timelines. Change roles if you must. Peace without edges turns into appeasement. Peace with edges turns into order. You are allowed to say I wish you well and I am stepping away.

Forgiveness supports this law, but they are not the same. Peace is the way you act in the world while forgiveness is the way you release the hook in your own chest. You can choose peaceful actions while you are still working on letting go inside. Keep moving both forward at a speed that honors your healing.

Teach this law to children and teams by making it visible. When someone makes a mess, model a clean response. Here is what happened. Here is how we make it right. Here is the rule that prevents a repeat. Speak in a steady voice. Show how accountability and care can live in the same sentence. People remember the tone more than the lecture.

Use a simple structure when the urge for payback rises. Name your aim. I want a just outcome. Name the standard. Here is the rule and the impact. Name the next step. Here is what I will do today. Then stop. Do not add a punishing extra. Do not send the late night message. Do not tell the story three more times. Protect your peace by ending the scene with a clear period.

Close with a practice you can use this week. Choose one situation that still pulls you toward payback. Write two columns. In the first, list the actions that would feel good for five minutes and harm you for five months. In the second, list the actions that would feel calm now and serve you later. Pick one item from the second column and do it. Send the factual summary. Set the boundary in writing. Return the keys. Withdraw from the thread. Then go for a short walk and breathe like a person who just chose their future.

Peace speaks louder than revenge because peace leaves a trail you can stand on. It holds your values. It lowers the noise. It invites better from others and it keeps your hands free to build what is next. Let your calm be your message. Let your follow through be your proof. The people who matter will hear you clearly. More important, you will hear yourself.

Law 19

Kindness Does Not Chase Recognition

Kindness is complete the moment you offer it. It does not look over its shoulder to see who is clapping. It does not keep a private ledger. It moves like water. It gives what is needed and then keeps moving. When you stop chasing recognition, your care becomes lighter and your life becomes calmer. You act from values instead of from a need to be seen.

Recognition is not wrong. It can be sweet and it can be useful. The trouble begins when approval becomes the fuel. Then every generous act turns into a test. Did they notice. Did they say thank you. Did they post about it. Your mood rises and falls on outcomes you do not control. Kindness is a steadier path. You choose the right act and you let the echo take care of itself.

At home this looks like simple service without a speech. You take out the trash because shared spaces are easier to love when they are cared for. You lay out a shirt for a sleepy child because mornings go better when small frictions are gone. You welcome a partner at the door with eye contact because beginnings shape nights. None of these need an announcement. The house feels your care whether or not anyone names it.

With friends, kindness that does not chase recognition protects the friendship from quiet bargains. You give a ride without expecting a matching favor. You listen without keeping score. If you need something, you say it plainly. Can you help me on Saturday. I would appreciate an hour. Clear asks are cleaner than hints. When you release the hunt for credit, your yes stays warm and your no stays honest.

At work, this law builds trust. You share the process that saves time. You credit people by name when their idea moves the project. You write a clear summary after a meeting so the next person can move without chasing you. You do these things because they make the work humane and effective. Praise may come. It may not. Either way, the culture rises and your reputation grows for reasons that last.

There is a quiet practice that keeps your heart aligned. Before you give, name your intention in one sentence. I am doing this to make the path easier. I am doing this because it is right. I am doing this so the team can think. Let the sentence be your reward. When applause arrives, enjoy it without needing it. When it does not, enjoy the clean feeling of acting from principle.

Kindness that does not chase recognition still holds boundaries. You are not a ghost. Your work matters. If credit is being misassigned in ways that harm results or careers, address it with clarity. Use facts. On slide three the approach came from Mei's test last week. Please keep her looped for decisions. Put contributions in writing. Keep your voice even. This is not fishing for praise. This is stewardship.

Your body will tell you when the need for recognition is tugging at you. You feel a small sting when someone else is thanked. You rehearse a story about your effort in your head. When you notice the tug, breathe once and return to your aim. Ask a better question. Did the outcome improve because I acted. If yes, let that answer feed you. If not, adjust the action next time so it truly serves.

Language helps you live this law without sounding performative. Keep your words short and plain. Happy to help. Here is what I can do. Here is what I learned. When praise comes, accept it with a simple thank you and pass the light where it belongs. The team did the heavy lift. That sentence builds more goodwill than any spotlight ever could.

Online, practice quiet generosity. Share a resource that helped you. Answer a question from a stranger with patience. Credit the source. Then move on. Do not look back to count likes. Your day is better when your giving is not tied to a scoreboard that changes by the hour.

There will be times when you are overlooked in ways that cost you opportunity. Kindness does not ask you to accept that. Advocate for yourself with calm documentation. Keep a one page record of your impact. Send a quarterly note with outcomes and next goals. Ask for the meeting you need. The

LAW 19

difference is tone. You are not asking to be praised. You are making sure the right information is on the table so the work can advance.

Teach this law at home and on teams by turning recognition outward. Say names in rooms of power. Tell the story of someone else's craft when it improves the day. People will feel safe around you because you are not competing for attention at all costs. Ironically, this is how your own name travels. Not because you chased it, but because you create spaces where credit flows.

Close with a small practice for the week. Choose one act of quiet generosity each day and do it without telling anyone. Wipe a counter that you did not dirty. Send a clear template that saves an hour. Leave a kind note where it will help. At night, write one line in your notes. I did this because it was right. Feel the clean weight of that sentence. It is enough.

Kindness does not chase recognition. It chooses meaning over display. It steadies your spirit and frees your time. It leaves rooms better than it found them and moves on. Let your work speak for you. Let your follow through be your proof. The people who matter will see. More important, you will see yourself clearly and like the person you are becoming.

Law 20

Do Not Bleed for Those Who Chose Their Wounds

Kindness is medicine. It is not a transfusion that drains you dry. Some people want relief with no change. They want your time, your money, your attention, and they want to keep the pattern that created the pain. This law asks you to keep your heart open and your eyes clear. Offer water, not life support. Give help that respects dignity and requires responsibility.

A chosen wound is a repeated cut that a person refuses to tend. You will hear the same story with new names. You will see the same emergency on a different day. When you offer a path, the steps are ignored. When you set a fair limit, outrage appears. Notice the pattern. Kindness without a boundary becomes fuel for the next spin.

Begin with consent and capacity. Ask yourself two questions. Do I have the energy to help well. Will my help support change rather than delay it. If either answer is no, you can still be kind without giving more of yourself. Wish them well. Offer one clear resource. Step back. Your peace is not a selfish prize. It is the ground that keeps your care honest.

At home, protecting your energy teaches everyone how to live. The teen who always forgets, the relative who always needs a loan, the partner who always runs late. Compassion sees stress. Wisdom sets structure. Write the rule in plain words. Tie privilege to follow through. Money comes with a written plan. Rides come after chores. Late arrivals reduce future invites. You are not punishing. You are refusing to keep bleeding for a wound that is being kept open.

With a partner, chosen wounds often hide in cycles. The apology is real, the change is not. Keep your softness and add proof. I want us to work. For the next ninety days we will use a shared calendar, a check in, and a rule for hard talks. If this slips, we will pause overnights or seek help. Love stays warm. Access becomes conditional on behavior. Your boundary protects both of you from a story that never ends.

At work, do not turn your calendar into a rescue service. There are colleagues who live in crisis. The deadline is always burning, the request is always last minute, the same blockers appear every sprint. Help once with a real fix. Write a playbook. Move decisions into one page. Schedule checkpoints. After that, replace endless saves with process. I can review if the draft arrives by noon. I will help scope, not carry. Calm structure is respect for the team and for your health.

Your body is a reliable alarm. Dread when a name pops up. A heavy sigh before you answer. A quick yes followed by resentment. Treat these sensations as information. Pause for one breath. Name the pattern out loud. This is the third time. I am about to spend energy that will not change the outcome. Then select a response that honors your limits.

Language helps. Keep a few sentences ready that sound like you.

· I care about you and I do not have capacity for this.

· Here is one resource that could help.

· I can offer thirty minutes and I will end on time.

· I will support if you do these two steps by Friday.

· I am not able to engage while you are speaking in that tone.

Say the line once in a steady voice. If it is tested, repeat once. Then exit.

Exiting is not cruelty. It is clarity. When you withdraw from a dynamic that feeds on your energy, you teach with your feet. You also create space where real help might be considered. Many people only face their pattern when the easy supply ends. Your soft no can be the beginning of their yes to change.

There is a difference between emergency and theater. In a true emergency, help if you safely can. Drive. Watch the child. Call the number. When the same alarm rings every week, it is not an emergency. It is design. Remove your part from the design.

Offer a checklist or a calendar. Put the plan in writing. If the pattern returns, decline and point back to the plan.

Generosity can still live here. You can be generous with clarity, with introductions, with templates that save time. You can be generous with one short call that sets direction instead of an all night rescue. You can be generous with a warm goodbye when someone refuses the terms that protect your life. Kindness is not measured by how much of yourself you give up. It is measured by how much dignity remains after you act.

Self care is not an apology. It is maintenance. Protect sleep. Keep quiet windows. Eat real food. Move your body. These basic choices make it possible to show up where your help can actually help. Without them, you will mistake guilt for responsibility and you will say yes when you mean no.

If guilt rises, check your aim. Are you protecting comfort, or are you protecting truth and growth. Comfort wants you to fix feelings. Truth wants you to support actions. You are allowed to choose truth. You are allowed to let people feel their feelings while you hold your line.

Try a simple practice for seven days. Choose one relationship that drains you. Write a short contract with yourself. What I can offer. What I will not offer. What proves progress. Share a version of it if needed. Then keep the contract for one week without explaining it over and over. Notice your energy. Notice whether the other person steps up when the free supply ends.

Do not bleed for those who chose their wounds. Offer clean care with clear boundaries. Support steps, not cycles. Walk with people who are walking. Pray or wish well for those who are not, and keep moving. Your life is not an endless reservoir for someone else's refusal to change. Your life is the vessel that carries your purpose, your home, and the people who are ready to heal. Guard it.

Law 21

What You Bless Expands

Blessing is focused goodwill. It is the habit of placing your attention on what you want to see grow and doing so with sincerity. You do not need incense or a ceremony. You need intention, words that are alive, and a steady practice. What you bless does not suddenly become perfect. It becomes supported. It receives light and structure. It receives your patience. Over time, that combination multiplies.

This law is not about pretending everything is fine. Blessing without truth is flattery. Blessing with truth is cultivation. You name what is real, even the hard parts, and you add your will for the good. Thank you for the progress we made and here is the next small step. I see your effort and here is the boundary that keeps us honest. Blessing paired with clarity teaches the world what to build and what to stop.

Begin with yourself. Many people try to bless others while starving their own spirit. Offer a quiet blessing each morning as you put your feet on the floor. May I move with clarity and care. May I keep dignity for myself and others. Follow it with one concrete act that proves you mean it. Drink water. Open a window. Write the top three tasks. Blessing needs behavior to take root.

At home, bless what you want to grow and watch how the room shifts. When a child tries, catch the effort, not only the result. I see how patient you were with that puzzle. Thank you for sticking with it. When a partner makes a small repair, make it visible. I noticed you reset the calendar. It helped my afternoon go smooth. This is not performance. It is placing light on seeds you want to see again.

Blessing at work looks like naming skill and pointing it toward the goal. After a meeting, send a two line note. Your summary made the decision simple. Please run our next check in the same way. Put credit in writing where power can see it. Use names. Use specifics. Do it without a speech. People will begin to repeat what is recognized. That is expansion in practice.

Your words are tools. Choose short phrases that carry steady warmth. May this conversation bring clarity and respect. May our team build with care. May my tone stay calm while I tell the truth. Say them quietly before you begin. You are not asking the world to be easy. You are choosing your stance. Your stance shapes outcomes more than you think.

Blessing can coexist with boundaries. You can bless a person's growth while limiting their access to you. You can bless a relationship and still insist on new rules. You can bless your community and still demand accountability. A strong boundary is often the most powerful blessing you can give. It tells the truth about what must change so love can live.

Use your body to deliver the message. When you bless, soften your face and breathe low. Let your shoulders fall. Speak at a pace that allows listeners to feel your meaning. Presence is part of the gift. People sense when goodwill is real because the body will not perform it for long if it is not.

Be careful with sarcasm. It is a kind of reverse blessing that shrinks what you touch. If you are tempted to undercut a moment, pause and ask what you fear. Often it is closeness or responsibility. Choose a cleaner line. Say less. Name the next step. Let the work speak.

Blessing does not replace repair. If harm happened, begin with truth and consequence. Then bless the path forward. I accept the apology. For the next month we will meet weekly and review the plan in writing. May we keep the standard and keep the tone kind. Now the blessing has rails. Without rails it slides into wishful thinking.

Bring blessing into the places that feel thin. Your commute. The inbox. The kitchen at night. Pick a small ritual. One song that settles you. One cup placed carefully in the cabinet. One note of thanks sent before you open the next message. The point is not to decorate your life. The point is to keep your heart from drying out. A hydrated heart is more effective than a harsh one.

If you are worried this is naive, measure it. For one week, bless the exact behaviors you want to see in one relationship and set one boundary that protects the effort. Track the results. Do conversations get shorter and cleaner. Do people take more ownership. Do you sleep better. If yes, continue. If not, refine. Bless fewer things with more specificity. Add a clearer edge. Make the next step smaller.

There is also a way to bless in silence. When you think of someone, send a quiet wish without texting. May they find the help they need. May they feel steadier today. This costs nothing and softens your own mind. It turns envy into gratitude. It turns comparison into peace. Your day opens because you are no longer feeding rivalries that do not serve you.

Children learn this quickly. Create a small practice at dinner or bedtime. What did you bless today. Keep the answers ordinary. A friend who shared. A teacher who tried a new method. The meal that tasted good. The habit forms. Children who learn to notice good without denying truth grow into adults who can build under pressure.

Close with a simple template you can use anywhere. Name the good. Name the next step. Add a short blessing. Our team finished the draft. Tomorrow we cut it by 20 percent. May we keep the core and let the rest go. Use this in your notes, in your meetings, and in your home. It keeps focus where growth can happen.

What you bless expands. Attention is water. Words are light. Boundaries are the garden walls. Give all three and watch your life become more orderly and more kind. You will notice that people relax near you. You will notice that the work moves. You will notice that your own spirit stays warm. That is the quiet power of this law.

Law 22

Keep Your Word Like Currency

A promise is not a sentence. It is an agreement with weight. When you give your word, you are spending from an account called trust. Spend carelessly and the account runs dry. Spend wisely and it grows interest you can use when life gets complicated. Kindness depends on this account. People relax around you when your word holds.

Start with simple honesty. Do not offer what you cannot deliver. It is kinder to say a clean no than a hopeful yes that collapses later. Before you agree, check three things. Do I have the time. Do I have the energy. Do I have the will. If any answer is no, offer a boundary or an alternative. I cannot take the whole task. I can review one page by Thursday. Clean terms protect both sides.

Clarity is part of the promise. A fuzzy yes creates disappointment. A precise yes creates relief. Put details in writing when it matters. What will be done, by whom, by when, and in what form. At home this can be as simple as I will pick up at three and text when I leave. At work it can be a one page note with owners and dates. Writing removes guesswork and lets everyone plan.

Your word includes tone. Say less and mean more. Over promising is often a hidden wish to be liked. The result is late nights, quiet resentment, and a reputation that looks shiny and then cracks. A modest promise delivered on time is worth more than a grand promise delivered with excuses. People remember the weight that held, not the size of the speech.

When you must break your word, repair like a professional. Move fast. Name the impact without defending yourself. I said Friday and I missed it. That created pressure for you. Here is what I have done and here is the new date. Ask what would help right now. Then meet the new promise exactly. A clean repair restores more trust than silence ever could.

Boundaries help you keep a good ledger. Protect focus time. Keep a short list of active commitments and review it daily. If new requests arrive, compare them to the list in front of you. Trade honestly instead of stacking until things fall. I can take this if we move the other item to next week. Kindness that keeps its word often looks like calm scheduling.

Teach children what a promise is by modeling it. Say what will happen in plain language and follow through. When plans must change, show them how to repair. I said we would go tonight. I am too tired to drive safely. I will take you tomorrow at ten. Let them see that a promise is a living thing that can be adjusted with truth and care.

In partnerships, keep small vows visible. I will not threaten to leave during an argument. I will not use old mistakes to win a point. I will tell you when my capacity is low. These are quiet promises that hold the room steady. When one is broken, acknowledge it and reset early. The relationship stays safe because words and behavior match again.

At work, treat deadlines as a way to honor people. A date is not only a project milestone. It is a promise to the lives behind it. To the person arranging childcare. To the client planning inventory. To the teammate who built their week around your handoff. When you deliver on time, you are saying I see you. When you cannot, you are saying I see you and I will not leave you guessing. That is leadership.

Your body will tell you when you are about to overspend your account. A quick yes at the edge of a meeting. A tight jaw when you open your calendar. A small drop in your stomach as you type sure. Pause for one breath and check your answers again. Time. Energy. Will. If you cannot pay in full, offer terms that you know you can keep.

Language keeps your word strong without sounding hard. Try lines like these.
· I can commit to this part by Wednesday. I need till noon to give you quality.

· I cannot take this on, and here are two options that may help.

·Thank you for trusting me with this.
Each sentence sets an honest shape. People will prefer a clear

limit to a warm promise that falls apart.

Credit is part of keeping your word too. If you promised to name the people who made the work possible, do it in public and do it accurately. Say their names in rooms of power. Include them on the email that reports the win. Your word about credit builds a culture where people want to build with you again.

Keep one eye on your promises to yourself. Self trust is the well that feeds every other vow. Choose small commitments you can keep on your worst day. Ten minutes of movement. One glass of water before coffee. No phone in the bedroom. Every time you keep a promise to yourself, your voice gains weight. People feel it even when you say little.

Close with a short practice for the week. Make a list of your current promises. Circle the ones that are vague. Turn each into one sentence with a clear deliverable and date. Send those sentences to the right people. If any promise is impossible, repair now with a new plan. Then protect three blocks on your calendar to deliver. At the end of the week, write what held and what slipped. Adjust your future yes accordingly.

Keep your word like currency. Spend it with care. Track it with clarity. Repair it with speed. When your promises hold, kindness becomes something people can lean on. Your presence calms rooms. Your name carries weight. And your life moves with a steady rhythm that feels good to live inside.

Law 23

Kindness Without Justice Breeds Harm

Kindness without justice is sugar on a crack. It tastes sweet for a moment and then the wall gives way. Real kindness protects the people in the room and the people who will enter after you. It tells the truth, sets the line, and follows through. When you skip justice, the same hurt repeats. When you marry kindness to justice, trust grows and peace lasts.

Justice is not rage. Justice is order that keeps dignity intact. It asks four questions. What happened. Who was affected. What repairs are needed. What guardrails will prevent a repeat. Answer in plain words. Then act. Your tone can stay warm. Your plan must be firm.

Mercy is beautiful when there is ownership and change. Mercy becomes harm when it removes consequence. Kindness can forgive a person and still protect the house. You can bless the future and still require proof today. This is not cruelty. This is stewardship.

At home, justice sounds like calm rules and clear repair. A child breaks a rule and you want to wave it away because you love their face. Love tells the truth. The paint is on the wall. The wall needs cleaning. The markers live in the cabinet. You teach the skill that prevents a repeat and you follow up tomorrow. The child learns that home is safe because feelings do not erase agreements.

With a partner, kindness without justice turns into resentment. You apologize to keep the peace, but the pattern returns. Replace hush with structure. Here is what happened. Here is how it landed. Here is the plan for next time. If the plan slips, access changes for a while. Fewer late nights. Shared calendar. Weekly check in. You keep your voice gentle and your boundary real. The relationship breathes because safety is not left to chance.

In friendship, kindness often tries to rescue. Justice protects both of you from a cycle. A friend repeats the same emergency and refuses the steps that would heal it. You can be kind and truthful. I care about you. I cannot keep doing midnight calls. I can talk tomorrow for twenty minutes. I can help you make the appointment. If the pattern continues, you step back and wish them well. That distance is not a sentence. It is a space where responsibility can grow.

At work, kindness without justice ruins teams. A deadline is missed. You feel bad and move on. The same issue returns and now five people pay the price. Choose justice with care. Write the facts on one page. Name the impact. Narrow scope. Set checkpoints with owners and dates. Offer help that builds skill, not dependence. If someone harms the culture through disrespect, address it early. Speak once in private with clear standards. Document. If it repeats, follow the process that exists. People will relax when they see that standards are not a mood.

Justice has a body. It shows up in how you stand and breathe. Before a hard talk, put both feet flat. Inhale through your nose for four. Hold for two. Exhale for six. Drop your shoulders one inch. This posture keeps your voice steady. Steady voices help people hear the line without feeling attacked. Justice delivered calmly is easier to accept and harder to argue with.

Language helps you hold both kindness and justice. Keep a few lines ready.
   Here is what happened and how it affected us.
   I care about you and I am not going to ignore this.
   Here is the repair that is needed and the time it is due.
   Here is the boundary that protects us while we rebuild trust.
   If this repeats, access will change.
   Thank you for doing your part.

Justice is not gossip. If a matter is private, keep it in the smallest room that can hold it. If a matter was public, include a public repair. Correct the record with facts. Thank the people who carried the extra weight. Close with next steps. Your aim is an honest outcome, not a show.

Kindness asks you to see power clearly. Protect the small. Give voice to the person who is often interrupted. Learn names and pronounce them with care. Pay on time. Credit by name. Write rules so even the newest person can appeal to them. A just room does not depend on a single generous mood. It depends on design.

Justice includes consequence. Consequence is not revenge. Revenge tries to hurt. Consequence teaches. It might be a change in role. It might be a pause on a privilege. It might be more supervision for a season. You set it with a steady hand and a clear reason. You lift it when the proof is real. No drama. Only design.

When you are the one who missed the mark, invite justice on yourself. Name the harm. Apologize. Ask what repair looks like. Offer a plan with dates. Accept the boundary that follows. Then show the change. You will rebuild faster because you chose the standard instead of dodging it.

If someone calls your boundary unkind, return to the measure. Does this choice protect dignity, including yours. Does it reduce future harm. If yes, keep the line. If no, adjust the shape. You are allowed to refine. Justice improves with practice.

Online, practice small just acts. Credit sources. Correct errors once with a link. Refuse to pile on. Report abuse where it belongs. Then log off. Your attention is a resource. Spend it where outcomes can improve.

Close the loop with grace when the work is done. After truth, boundary, and consequence, you can end with a simple blessing. We are complete. Try again tomorrow. Grace is not a shortcut. It is the last step that keeps your spirit light.

A short practice for this week. Choose one place where kindness has been covering a crack. Write three lines. The fact. The impact. The needed repair. Speak them in a warm, steady voice to the right person. Set one boundary that protects everyone while the repair happens. Put a date on the calendar to check progress. When the date comes, look at proof, not promises. If the repair is real, bless it and restore access. If it is not, extend the boundary or change the role. Keep your tone kind. Keep your plan strong.

Kindness without justice breeds harm. Kindness with justice builds homes, teams, and lives that can carry weight. Tell the truth. Hold the line. Choose repairs that teach. End with grace. This is how your care becomes safe to stand under. This is how peace lasts.

Law 24

Presence Heals Faster Than Advice

Some comforts work before a single word is spoken. A lamp already lit. A chair pulled close. A warm mug set within reach. When the room is arranged with care, the heart understands it can rest. Presence works the same way. It is the soft climate that lets truth breathe. Advice has its hour, but presence changes the air right now.

Advice is tempting because it feels useful. It gives our hands something to do and our mouths something to say. Yet a person in pain is often carrying a flooded nervous system, not a shortage of information. They do not need a map before they have a coat. Presence is the coat. It steadies the body so the mind can think again. Then the right next step reveals itself without force.

Begin like a good host. Lower your voice. Slow your pace. Offer water before wisdom. Sit at an easy angle so the person does not feel cornered. Keep your hands where they can be seen. Let silence be part of the welcome. Silence tells the truth about safety. It says there is no rush and no performance required.

At home, practice a two minute arrival. When someone walks in tired or tender, do not leap to the autopsy of the day. Greet them by name. Meet their eyes. Touch the table with your fingertips and breathe once together. Ask one simple question that makes room. Do you want comfort or a plan. If they want comfort, stay close and keep your words light. If they want a plan, write three steps and put the first on the calendar. Presence chooses sequence that fits the moment.

With children, presence looks like lowering to their height and naming what you see. Your shoulders are up. Your eyes are shiny. That was a big feeling. Sit with me. A soft lap and a warm washcloth will often do what speeches cannot. When the storm passes, offer one clean line. Next time we will try it this way. The lesson lands because the child never had to defend their dignity.

At work, presence is a craft. It reads the room before it speaks. It opens meetings with purpose and ends them with owners and dates so no one has to guess. In the middle, it listens all the way through and then reflects what it heard. Here is what matters, here is what helps. That short summary is presence doing its quiet repair. People leave steadier, which means they do better work.

Your body is the first instrument. Unclench your jaw. Lower your shoulders. Place both feet on the floor. Breathe in to a slow count of five and out to a slow count of five. This is not decoration. It is a signal that tells the other person they are near a steady shore. When your body is calm, your sentences shorten and soften. Advice becomes a simple next step instead of a speech.

Language can carry presence when you need it. Use lines that make space. I am here. Take your time. Tell me where it hurts most. Let me know when you want ideas. These phrases are small doors that do not creak. They protect the choice of the person who is hurting, which is part of healing.

Digital life needs this more than ever. Not every hard thing belongs in a group thread. Move tender topics to smaller rooms. Suggest a brief call so tone can be heard. If time zones or schedules do not allow a call, send a short voice note that begins with warmth and ends with one clear action. Even through a screen, presence is felt in pacing and care.

Presence is not the same as agreement. You can be steady and still set a line. If the conversation turns sharp, say I want a good outcome. I will continue when the tone is respectful. If the story repeats without change, say I care about you. I can listen for twenty minutes today. Then I need to return to my tasks. Boundaries keep presence from dissolving into exhaustion.

If you offered advice too soon, repair is simple. I moved to solving before I really heard you. I am sorry. Tell me again. Then listen without reaching for the tool belt. Trust that the other person carries wisdom that will rise once they feel safe. Your patience invites that wisdom to the table.

Small rituals make presence easy to reach. Keep a clean corner where hard talks can land. Light a candle before you begin and blow it out when both people feel heard. Place a pitcher of water and two glasses on the counter during family gatherings. Agree that phones rest on a tray for the first ten minutes after everyone comes home. These habits are little lanes that guide the evening toward gentleness.

When a friend is grieving, presence becomes food, rides, folded laundry, and quiet company. Advice is rarely needed and often unhelpful. Grief is a long road. Set a reminder to check in after the first week, the first month, the holidays that will sting. A note that says I am thinking of you turns the lights back on for a moment. That is what presence does. It brings light without demanding a performance.

Before you close this chapter, practice a small exchange. Think of someone you love. Picture what presence would look like in their next hard hour. A blanket by the couch. A cup of tea. A slow walk around the block. Decide your first sentence now and tuck it in your pocket. You will be ready when the door opens.

Presence heals faster than advice because it treats the real wound first. It calms the body. It honors dignity. It gives the heart a chance to loosen its grip so wisdom can do its work. Keep the lamp warm. Keep the chair close. Keep your words soft and your attention steady. The people you love will find their breath again, and then the next step will feel possible.

Law 25

Protect the Small

Power shows itself in how you treat what cannot benefit you. Anyone can be kind upward. Real character appears in hallways, in kitchens, at loading docks, and in quiet threads where there is no applause. Protecting the small is not sentimental. It is structural. It sets the tone of a house, a team, and a life. When the smallest feel safe, everyone can do their best work.

Small can mean many things. A child who is still learning. A junior teammate who does not yet have a voice in the room. A caregiver who is tired. A cashier on a long shift. A rule that seems minor but keeps people safe. A moment that could be dismissed and yet carries real weight. Protecting the small means noticing these places and choosing care with precision.

Begin at home. The way you correct a child teaches them what power is for. Lower your voice. Name the fact and the next step. The paint is on the table. We are going to clean with warm water and a sponge. Then teach the skill that prevents the repeat. A gentle correction now prevents a hard shame later. Pets are part of this law too. Feed on time. Keep fresh water. Children watch how you treat a creature that can give you nothing back except trust.

With a partner, protect the small details that keep love steady. Return texts when you say you will. Keep the shared calendar accurate. Announce changes early. These are not chores for their own sake. They are railings that prevent people from falling. When daily life has railings, difficult conversations are not as sharp because no one is walking on an edge.

In friendship, protect the small by keeping confidences and honoring thresholds. If a friend whispers I am at my limit, believe them. Do not press for a longer call. Do not turn their story into your content. You will become the person they can call because you do not turn need into spectacle.

At work, the small are often invisible. The receptionist who calms the building. The cleaner who resets the room. The intern who catches details. Notice and protect them. Learn names. Say thank you in ways that matter. Lift their concerns with the same seriousness you give to a client. When a meeting turns sharp, step in with one calm line that returns respect to the space. I want everyone to be able to finish a sentence. Protecting the small includes the person who made a first mistake. Correct firmly and keep dignity intact so growth remains possible.

Protect time as a small thing with large consequences. Start and end meetings when you said you would. Send a brief summary so no one has to guess. Cancel early if the purpose has changed.

Time is the resource that juniors cannot defend and seniors often waste without meaning to. When leaders guard time, the whole culture settles.

Language is a tool for this law. Speak to the quiet person in the room with direct questions that help them participate. What are we missing from your view. If someone is interrupted, return the floor without drama. I want to hear them finish. When you make an introduction, include the detail that builds credibility. Maria ran the pilot that got us to green. Small words change whether a person is heard.

Design is protection. Put the policy in writing so anyone can appeal to the rule rather than to you. Document decisions where all roles can see them. Build checklists that prevent the newest person from carrying the blame for a system gap. Good design lowers the temperature everywhere, especially for people who have the least ability to push back.

Money and credit are tests. Pay fairly and on time. When budgets are thin, do not save by cutting the pay of the least powerful. Cut noise first. Cut spectacle first. Credit is free and changes lives. Put names on slides where ideas began. Include authors on documents. Say who set the domino that led to the win. Those sentences cost seconds and build a more honest room.

Protecting the small includes how you handle harm. If someone is targeted, move quickly and calmly. Offer safety first. Separate people if needed. Record what happened in simple language. Use the process that already exists, and if it does not exist, create one. Consequence without cruelty keeps the culture sturdy and tells future harm that it will not find a home here.

Your body is part of this practice. Slow your pace in spaces where others cannot move as fast. Hold doors. Give the stroller or the cane the path without a flourish. Look people in the eye when you thank them. A steady presence communicates that everyone belongs. Small courtesies are not decoration. They are signals that the space is safe.

Online, protect the small by refusing to pile on. Add a clarifying source once if it will reduce harm and then log off. Do not share images of private people without consent. If you use community knowledge, credit the forum or the maker. Influence that does not protect its sources withers. Influence that shelters the small becomes trusted.

Beware of savior habits. Protecting the small does not mean removing all struggle. It means creating fair conditions and refusing humiliation. Ask clean questions. What would help. What can I move out of your way. What do you want to keep doing yourself. Then support without taking over. Dignity grows when people are treated as capable.

There will be days when this feels slow. It is not slow. It is durable. The rooms you build by protecting the small will save time later because there is less repair. Fewer apologies. Fewer rehires. Less turnover. More honest talk. More good work. More rest at night because you led in a way you can respect.

Try a short practice this week. Each morning choose one small thing to guard. Pronounce a name correctly and ask once if you are unsure. Send a thank you that includes the impact line. Offer a junior person the first slot to present. Replace what you finished in the shared drawer. At night, write one line on what changed because you did it. The changes will look small at first. Give it a month and watch the tone of your days shift.

Protect the small. That is power's test. Use your reach to build railings. Use your voice to return respect. Use your attention to make truth visible. When the smallest are safe, the whole house holds.

Law 26

Use Words To Build, Not Perform

Words are tools. They can frame a door so people can walk through, or they can create a stage where nothing useful happens. Performance asks to be admired. Building asks to be understood. When you use words to build, conversations become bridges. People know what is true, what matters, and what happens next.

The first measure of a building word is purpose. Ask yourself, what do I want this sentence to accomplish. Do I want to clarify, invite, decide, or repair. If the answer is I want to be seen, pause. You can be seen through your follow through. Let your language carry work, not applause.

Clarity is kindness in motion. Short, specific words respect the listener's time and nervous system. Replace drama with direction. Instead of This is always a disaster, try Here is the part that failed and here is how we will test the fix. The second line lowers the temperature and raises the quality of attention.

At home, building words turn small frictions into simple tasks. A child ignores a chore and you feel your voice getting sharp. Performance makes a speech. Building gives a path. The towels are on the floor. Hang them now and put the basket in the closet. Afterward, thank the effort you asked for. Thank you for finishing quickly. This loop keeps the house gentle and clear.

With a partner, building words protect closeness. Performance tries to win. Building tries to connect. Instead of You never listen, try When I am interrupted, I feel dismissed. I need you to let me finish and I will do the same for you. The message is firm and workable. The tone keeps dignity for both people.

At work, building language saves hours. Start meetings with the aim, the decision needed, and the owner. Speak to the problem, not the personalities. If tension rises, write on a board so the room can look at the same facts. Performance hunts for a clever line. Building hunts for the next useful step. When you close, send one short note that names owners, dates, and links. Good words finish what the room started.

Your body helps your words build. Slow your breath. Keep your shoulders down. Let your jaw unclench. Speak at a pace that allows the other person to think. A warm, steady voice carries more weight than fast talk. People hear you better when their nervous systems do not feel chased.

Timing decides whether words build or break. Truth spoken in a storm often becomes another storm. Wait for a moment when calm is possible, then speak the same truth with a plan attached. I want this to work. Here is what happened. Here is what I will do and here is what I need from you. Now the conversation has walls and a roof.

Use plain language. Jargon performs. Plain words invite. Say what you mean in sentences that anyone could repeat. If the topic is complex, stack your ideas like bricks. One idea per line, then mortar them together with a short summary. Do not confuse density with depth. Depth is accuracy and relevance that a tired person can still use.

Credit others with care and precision. Performance flatters. Building names the real work. This approach came from Sam's test. The timeline held because Joy cleared the blockers. Specific credit teaches the room what to repeat and who to trust. It also keeps envy out because the facts are on record.

Boundaries belong in building talk. You can be clear without being cruel. Use lines that hold shape without heat. I cannot take that on, and here are two options. I will discuss this when voices are calm. We agreed to this date. If it changes, another deadline moves. Short limits prevent long arguments.

Online, building words are rare and powerful. Add value once. Offer a source. Ask a clean question. If the thread turns performative, leave. Your energy is too valuable to feed a show. Silence can be a structural choice. It keeps you available for work that matters.

When you miss the mark, repair with the same tools. I performed instead of building. Here is the information I should have given. Here is the plan. A clean repair restores more trust than a shining paragraph ever will. People remember how quickly you returned to purpose.

Keep a small set of phrases that build by default. I want to understand. Here is the decision we need. Here is what I can offer today. What would help most right now. Thank you for the part you did. Practice them out loud so they feel natural under pressure. In tense moments we do not rise to our hopes. We fall to our habits. Make these your habits.

Teach this law to children and teams by making it visible. Post the aim of the day where all can see it. Label shared drawers and return items to their places. Write the steps of a recurring task so no one has to ask you twice. Each label is a sentence made of tape and ink. It builds the room without a speech.

Measure your results. After you choose building words, do shoulders drop. Do decisions get made. Does sleep come easier. If yes, you are on the right track. If not, lower your word count, raise your specificity, and add a next step you can complete within the day. Adjust until your language reliably produces calm movement.

A practice to end. Before your next important exchange, write three lines. Aim. Fact. Next step. Say them in a warm, steady voice. Then stop talking and let the other person respond. You will notice that clarity invites clarity. Work moves. Rooms relax.

Use words to build, not perform. Choose purpose over theater, truth over noise, and direction over display. You will waste less time, protect more dignity, and leave conversations with more finished than when you began.

Law 27

Chapter 27. Choose Repair Over Punishment

Punishment is quick. It looks decisive and it can feel satisfying for a minute. Repair is slower and steadier. It moves a moment toward learning, safety, and trust. Kindness chooses repair because it asks the right question. What will make this better tomorrow. When you choose repair, you protect dignity and you protect results.

Punishment focuses on the person. It labels and shames. Repair focuses on the harm. It names what happened, who was affected, and what will be made right. This shift does not remove consequences. It makes consequences useful. People remember what they practice. Let them practice the skills that prevent a repeat.

Begin at home. A child breaks a rule. Instead of a long lecture, use a clean order. State the fact. State the impact. State the repair. The markers are on the wall. The wall needs cleaning and the markers go in the cabinet. Then teach the skill that was missing. Show where paper lives. Practice asking before using supplies. The child learns to clean up, to ask, and to respect shared space. The house stays gentle and clear.

With a partner, punishment often shows up as cold tone or a scorecard. It creates distance and invites performance rather than honesty. Repair sounds like this. Yesterday hurt. Here is what happened and here is how it landed. I would like a different plan for next time. What can we try. Now you are building a path back to trust. If a pattern continues, repair grows a firmer edge. Access shifts. Check ins appear. The tone stays warm while the plan becomes real.

At work, repair preserves people and standards at the same time. A deadline slips. Punishment shames the person in public and calls it accountability. Repair puts facts on one page, narrows scope, and sets checkpoints with owners and dates. It asks what blocked the work and which block belongs to design rather than to a single person. It invites the person who missed to help write the fix. People rise under that kind of structure because it treats them like adults who can learn.

Repair requires clarity. Be specific about the harm and the needed action. Vague apologies and vague plans will not hold. Keep words simple and precise. Here is what missed. Here is the effect. Here is the repair and the time it is due. Here is the guardrail that prevents a repeat. Write it down. Send it. When people see the steps, they can walk them.

Your body can help you choose repair. Punishment burns hot. It speeds your speech and tightens your jaw. When you feel heat rise, pause for a single minute. Inhale through your nose for four counts. Hold for two. Exhale for six. Drop your shoulders. Now speak. Your voice will be steadier and your words will be shorter. That combination invites responsibility rather than defense.

Repair includes apology when it belongs to you. Model it. Say the thing plainly. I raised my voice. That was not respectful. Here is what I will do next time. Then make a visible change. People learn more from the repair you perform than from the standards you announce.

Boundaries and repair are twins. Repair without boundaries becomes enabling. Boundaries without repair become punishment. Hold both. If someone breaks an agreement, access can change while repair proceeds. Fewer late night calls. More written decisions. A pause in privileges while skills are built. No venom. Only design.

Language is a tool for this law. Keep a few sentences close that fit your voice.
   Here is what happened and how it affected us.
   Here is what we will do to make it right.
   Here is the check in where we confirm it holds.
   I want a better future more than a perfect apology.
   Thank you for doing your part of the repair.

If someone rejects the idea of repair and wants only punishment or only escape, stay steady. Repeat the offer once. Then set your line. I am available for repair. I am not available for blame or denial. If they refuse, act on your boundary and step away. You can wish them well and still protect your peace.

In community life, repair means centering those affected and making amends that matter. If trust was broken in public, the repair includes a public piece. If harm cost time or money, repayment is part of the plan. If the issue came from a system gap, fix the system. A single person should not carry blame for a design that made the mistake likely.

Online, choose repair by limiting how much you feed the spectacle. If you correct something, cite a clear source and suggest a next step. Do not pile on. Do not perform outrage for strangers. Log off and put your care where you can touch the outcome.

There will be times when punishment feels cleaner. It is not. It is only faster. Repair gives you a future that does not run on fear. Homes get calmer. Teams get smarter. You get your sleep back because you built a process that holds after the talk ends.

End with a small practice you can use today. Think of a place where punishment shows up in your life. Write two short scripts. One for the moment of heat and one for the plan. For the moment of heat, use a single line. I am going to speak when I can be clear. For the plan, write three sentences. Here is the harm. Here is the repair. Here is when we check. Use the scripts once this week. Notice the difference in tone and in outcome.

Choose repair over punishment. Tell the truth, protect dignity, and move the moment toward learning. Over time this choice builds people who can own their part, fix what they broke, and keep building with you. That is the kind of strength that lasts.

Law 28

Honor Your Vessel First

Warm homes begin with warm bodies. Before the pies and the place cards, before the plans and the pep talks, there is the person who lights the candle and fills the kettle. That person is you. Your body and your nervous system are the house of your kindness. If you care for them first, every good thing you mean to give arrives whole. If you do not, even your best intentions come out thin. An empty cup only spills dust.

Think of yourself as a kitchen in winter. The stove needs fuel. The counters need a quick wipe so there is room to work. The window needs to open for a breath of fresh air. None of this is indulgence. It is preparation. When you feed the fire properly, one flame can warm the whole room. If you starve it, everyone shivers.

Rest is the first ingredient. Real rest, the kind that closes the door on noise and lets your bones remember that they are held. Choose a bedtime that respects tomorrow and treat it like a promise, not a wish. Dim the lights, wash your face slowly, put your phone to sleep where it cannot tug at you. If worries start their parade, write three lines on a card for morning. Your body will settle when it knows your mind has a plan.

Food is kindness that can be tasted. Eat in a way that keeps your hands steady. Simple meals count. Eggs with salt and pepper. Soup with a heel of bread. Apples sliced and shared. Sit for a few minutes, even if the day is busy. Sitting says you are a person, not a passing tray. When you nourish yourself on purpose, you speak a language your nervous system understands. Safe. Steady. Ready.

Water is a small miracle that most of us forget. Keep a glass within reach the way you keep a towel by the sink. Sip before hard conversations. Sip when tempers rise. Sip when grief visits. It is hard to be kind with a dry mouth and a tight jaw. Warm tea can soften a house faster than a hard speech ever could.

Breath is the quiet tool you always carry. If a moment turns sharp, place all ten fingertips on the table so your mind remembers where you are. Inhale to a slow count of five, exhale to a slow count of five. Shoulders down, jaw soft, feet planted. This is not decoration. It is a reset that tells your whole system that you are safe enough to choose your tone. Your words will come out warmer when your breath leads the way.

Movement is a hedge against harshness. Walk around the block. Stretch while the kettle hums. Put on a song you love and let your body sway while you fold towels. None of this needs to be grand. The goal is circulation, not performance. When your blood moves, patience moves with it. The first person to benefit is the one who will speak next to you.

Honor your vessel with boundaries that protect your peace. Decide when work ends and keep the ending gentle and visible. Close the laptop, wipe the counter, light a lamp. Tell people you love what your evening looks like so they can work with your rhythm instead of against it. A boundary is not a wall. It is a gate that keeps the garden healthy.

Watch for your tells. Your body will whisper before it shouts. Maybe your shoulders creep up. Maybe your breath gets thin. Maybe you reach for a screen when you are not truly looking for information. When you notice the sign, step into a tiny ritual. Rinse your hands in warm water. Sit for one minute with your eyes near a window. Eat something that grows on a tree. These moves are small and human. They return you to yourself.

Do not measure self care by perfection. Measure it by honesty. Some days the best you can do is a napkin folded neatly and a glass of water. Good. Claim it. Other days you will have room for a walk, a hot bath, a phone call with a friend who steadies you. Claim that too. What matters is the message beneath the act. I keep myself in good working order so my love can be trustworthy.

If guilt arrives, treat it like a guest who misunderstood the invitation. You are not choosing yourself instead of others. You are choosing the version of yourself that can be kind without breaking. Say it out loud if you have to. I am going to bed so tomorrow's me can be generous. Then go.

LAW 28

Teach the people around you to honor your vessel by showing them how it is done. Children learn that adults who rest are kinder. Partners learn that clear routines make a home easier to live in. Colleagues learn that your yes means yes because you do not trade sleep for promises. You will be surprised how quickly the house follows when you keep this tone.

There will be seasons of real strain. New babies. Illness. Deadlines that crowd the calendar. In those times, shrink the practice but keep the principle. Two more sips of water. Three deeper breaths. A ten minute lie down. A short walk to the mailbox. A sandwich at a table rather than over the sink. The smallest honors still count.

Before you close this chapter, choose one kindness for your body that you will keep for seven days. A glass of water at waking. A bedtime that arrives at the same hour. A short stretch before dinner. Write it on a card and place it where your hand will find it. Tell one person who will cheer you on. Then notice how your voice changes when your body feels cared for.

Honor your vessel first. The house of your kindness needs fuel, light, and rest. Give them without apology. You will find that your patience lasts longer, your boundaries hold better, and your love keeps its flavor from morning to night. That is how a life becomes a soft place for others to land, and a safe place for you to stand.

Law 29

Protect Your Quiet Windows

Quiet windows are the intervals when your mind can return to center and your spirit can refill. They can be ten minutes in the morning, an hour after lunch, or a short walk at dusk. These windows are not a luxury. They are maintenance. When you protect them, you protect every other law in this book. Your patience lasts longer. Your boundaries hold. Your words land softer because your nervous system has time to settle.

Quiet is not the same as isolation. Isolation pulls away from life. Quiet turns toward life with steadiness. In a quiet window you are present without pressure. You are letting the noise fall out of your muscles so your attention can choose where to go. Most mistakes of tone happen when we try to be generous on an empty tank. Quiet windows refill the tank.

Begin by noticing when your energy is naturally strongest and when it dips. Some people think clearly before the world wakes. Others find their focus after lunch once the morning dust has settled. Choose one or two times that fit your body. Claim them as windows where you do not scroll, explain, or perform. You breathe, write, read, plan, or simply sit. Small is enough. Ten minutes done daily changes more than an hour that never comes.

At home, make these windows simple and visible. Put water by the sink the night before and drink it quietly as the day starts. Stand by the window for one minute and let your eyes go wide so your body knows there is light. If you live with others, name your window in a warm voice. I am going to be quiet for the next fifteen minutes. I will help after that. Children learn quickly when the line is gentle and consistent. A closed door is clearer than a frustrated parent.

With a partner, quiet windows protect closeness. It sounds backward, but it is true. When both people have space to reset, the shared time is easier to enjoy. Trade morning or evening windows if your schedules overlap. Say what you will do with the time so it feels real rather than like a retreat. I will stretch and make a small list. I will sit outside without my phone. This removes guesswork and worry.

At work, guard quiet windows with structure. Put focus blocks on your calendar and treat them like meetings with your future self. Start the block with an entry ritual so your brain understands the shift. Close extra tabs. Put your phone in a drawer. Write the single sentence that describes the task. End the block with a small exit ritual. Note what you finished and what comes next. Send any decisions that unblock others so your quiet time supports the team.

Quiet windows need edges or the world will keep walking through them. Edges can be a sign on the door, a status light, or an auto reply that says when you will return. Edges can also be agreements. I do not take calls in this window unless it is urgent. I will answer messages at noon and four. When you keep your word to your own calendar, others begin to keep it too.

Your body is part of this law. Use short habits that settle you quickly. Plant both feet on the floor. Inhale for four counts. Hold for two. Exhale for six. Let your shoulders fall one inch. Keep your eyes soft. These cues tell your nervous system that you are safe. In two minutes the tone in your head will change. You will feel less pulled. You will hear your own intention again.

Technology can help if you set it up on purpose. Turn off nonessential alerts. Create a focus mode that allows only a few people to reach you. Put restful apps on your home screen and push the noisy ones to a second page. Try a ten minute sand timer on your desk. When the sand runs out, you stand up, drink water, and decide whether to extend or end the window. Tools should be servants, not supervisors.

Expect some pushback at first, especially if you have trained people to get instant access to you. Stay kind and repeat your line. I am in a focus window. I will respond at noon. If someone takes offense, add one more sentence. I want to be thoughtful for you, not just fast. Then keep your promise and reply on time. Consistency turns resistance into respect.

When life is heavy, quiet windows are not a refusal to help. They are how you stay able to help. If a true emergency arrives, you will know. You will go. When patterns of pretend emergency arrive, your window will help you see them clearly. Quiet time reduces the fog that keeps you saying yes when you mean no.

If a window gets interrupted, repair it without drama. Step outside. Breathe once. Decide what the next smallest quiet step can be. Two minutes with your eyes closed. A single paragraph in your notebook. Washing a few dishes with warm water. Small repairs keep the day from unraveling because you never wait for perfect conditions to reset.

Language supports this practice. Keep phrases that are clear and warm. I will be offline until ten and will reply after. I am in a thinking block. I will circle back at two. I want to give you quality, so I am stepping into quiet and will follow up by end of day. Use the same approach at home. I am going to read for fifteen minutes. I will be with you after that. The words are simple. The tone is steady.

Measure your results so you believe in the habit. After one week of protecting two small windows a day, ask three questions. Did my pace feel calmer. Did my corrections become kinder. Did my decisions hold better. If yes, keep the windows. If not, change the time or the shape. Make them shorter. Move them to a place with more light. Add a short walk or a cup of tea. Adjust until the window feeds you.

Close with a practice you can start tonight. Set a timer for eight minutes. Sit where you can see a piece of sky, even if it is small. Put your phone face down. Breathe and let your jaw unclench.

Write one sentence that names your aim for tomorrow. Then write the first step. When the timer ends, tidy one surface. You have just created and completed a quiet window. Protect it again tomorrow. Over time these windows will hold your days together. They will make you kinder without trying.

Law 30

Return What You Take

Kindness is a circle. Whatever you take from the circle should come back to it. If you borrow a tool, return it clean. If you ask for time, give back clarity. If you take trust, bring back proof that it was safe with you. Returning what you take keeps relationships whole. It keeps communities sturdy. It keeps your name light.

There are many kinds of borrowing. We borrow objects and spaces. We borrow attention when we talk through our worries. We borrow culture when we use ideas or traditions that others built. We borrow momentum when we step onto projects already in motion. Each kind asks for a fitting return. The return does not have to be grand. It does have to be sincere and specific.

Start with the easy versions. If you used something, give it back a little better. Rinse the bowl. Charge the battery. Replace the tape before the dispenser is empty. Small returns teach people that life gets easier after you pass through. The house breathes because you are in it.

Time is a delicate loan. When someone gives you an hour, honor the hour. Arrive on time. Know your aim. End when you said you would. Follow with a short note that names the decision or the next step. If they saved you from a mistake, tell them how their help changed the outcome. Returning time as clarity is one of the cleanest forms of care.

Trust is the largest loan. People hand you their stories and their reputations. Return trust with confidentiality and accuracy. Do not embellish what they told you. Do not repeat it where it does not belong. When you speak for a person in a room they cannot enter, use the same care you would want for yourself. Say what you know. Say what you do not know. Put your name behind the part you can own. Trust grows when people learn that their truth comes back whole.

Culture is also a loan. Ideas, phrases, recipes, and styles have makers and homes. When you use what is not originally yours, bring it back better by crediting the source and by learning the context. Say the name in your caption. Invite the origin into the room when decisions and budgets are made. If you profit, share that profit. This is not politics. It is table manners for a shared world.

At home, returning what you take looks like replacing the toilet paper, refilling the ice tray, and putting the lid back on the jar. It looks like giving your partner quiet after they gave you a long listen. It looks like thanking the child who fed the dog and asking if they want to choose the playlist for dinner. You are teaching a rhythm where giving and receiving are not arguments. They are how the house runs.

With friends, be generous in both directions. If a friend moves you across town, show up for their craft fair or their first show. If someone covered you when money was tight, repay on schedule or create a plan and stick to it. If they gave you the name that opened a door, send them a clear note about how it went and say their name when you tell the story. Friendship stays light when every borrow is followed by a visible return.

At work, return what you take by closing loops. You borrowed attention in a meeting. Send the summary. You borrowed a teammate's expertise. Credit them in the update and ask if they want to walk the room through the detail. You borrowed runway from a manager. Deliver on the date or repair the slip early with a plan that respects the cost of the delay. People do their best work near colleagues who give back more order than they take.

Your body can help you keep this law. A small twinge of guilt when you pass the empty printer tray is a cue. You took the last pages. Return them. A heaviness after a long vent is a cue. You took emotional room. Return calm by doing a task that lifts weight off the person who listened. Put dinner on the table. Send the email you were avoiding. Action is a repayment.

Language keeps returns clear. Use short honest lines. Thank you for the hour. Here is what I decided. I borrowed your drill. It is on your porch with a new bit. You introduced me to the client. I named you in the meeting and looped you for the next phase. These sentences place the return on record. They also protect relationships from the quiet wear of unspoken debt.

Sometimes you cannot return in kind. That is fine. Return in value. If you cannot repay money today, repay with a transparent plan and reliable check ins. If you cannot carry the box, carry the calendar. If you cannot share a contact, share a playbook. People do not need perfect symmetry. They need to feel that you care about balance.

There will be moments when you forget. Repair quickly and without a performance. I kept your book too long. I am sorry. Here it is with a note. If you damaged something, replace it without being asked. If you missed a credit, correct it in the same place where the miss happened. The repair is part of the return. Done cleanly, it can deepen trust rather than shrink it.

This law applies to the future too. We borrow ease from tomorrow when we leave messes today. Return what you took by resetting the room before you sleep. Clear the counter. Write tomorrow's top three. Place the keys where they belong. You will wake inside a return you already made, and your day will start with kindness you sent ahead.

Try a simple practice for one week. Each night write three lines. What did I borrow. What did I return. What needs a return tomorrow. Then do one return before bed. Send the thank you. Put gas in the car. Credit the source in your post. Watch how your life grows quieter. Watch how the people around you soften. Returning what you take is a quiet way to bless the spaces that hold you.

LAW 30

Return what you take. Bring things back clean

Law 31

Credit Is Public Kindness

Credit is how kindness learns to travel. It is the part of generosity that you say out loud so other people can see the path that brought them here. When you name the hands that lifted the work, you turn a private thank you into a public signal. People learn who to trust. Opportunities find the right doors. The room becomes fairer and calmer because truth is on the record.

Private gratitude matters. Public credit multiplies. A quiet text keeps a bond warm. A sentence in the meeting notes moves careers. When you include names near decisions, budgets, and praise, you do more than compliment. You repair a place that often forgets to remember. The result is not only moral. It is practical. People work better when they know their effort will be seen.

Begin with accuracy. Credit belongs to the person who did the work, not to the loudest voice near the work. Say the name. Say the action. Say the impact. Mei found the bug that unblocked deployment. Darren wrote the draft that shaped the final message. Amina's call saved the client relationship. Short. Specific. Verifiable. This style respects everyone's time while it protects the truth.

At home, credit teaches dignity. Children grow faster when they hear what they did well and why it helped. You sorted the mail and the table looks calm. Thank you. Partners feel safer when their everyday labor is visible. I saw you reset the calendar. My afternoon went smooth because of that. Credit is oxygen for the invisible work that keeps a family going.

In friendship, credit removes quiet bargains. You do not hint at how much you do. You say simple words when a friend shows up. You drove me when my car broke down. That was a gift. Let me treat lunch. It is easier to keep a friendship balanced when the ledger is honest in both directions.

At work, make credit part of the process. Put contributors in the first paragraph of updates. In slides, label the source of data on the same page. In emails, name the person who supplied the key insight before you explain the choice. When you present, point to the person in the room who can answer deep questions because they built the thing. This is not performance. It is good design for complex work.

Give credit across lines of role, seniority, and style. Many rooms reward the presenter and ignore the builder. Correct that habit. Say the builder's name in front of people with power. Invite them to speak to one detail. They do not need to become a performer. They deserve to be visible. Over time the team learns that the path to recognition is contribution, not theater.

Your body can carry this law. Turn your shoulders toward the person you are crediting. Use their name with ease. Keep your voice level so the moment feels normal rather than rare. When credit is everyday, people stop scrambling for it. They focus on the work and on each other.

Be careful with flattery. Flattery is vague and often transactional. Credit is specific and free of hidden requests. Flattery tries to get something. Credit gives what is due. The difference is felt at once. People relax near the second one because it does not pull on them.

Credit has edges. You can celebrate someone and still name the standard. This piece was late, and when it arrived the analysis was strong. Thank you for the depth. Next time we need both the depth and the date. Praise does not erase truth. Truth does not cancel praise. Holding both teaches excellence without humiliation.

Language helps. Keep a few lines ready. This idea began with Priya's sketch on Tuesday. The customer story came from Luis. The final polish is Kendra's. If you worry that you will forget, make a small habit. After any meeting, write three names and one sentence for each. Put those sentences into the follow up. Five minutes of discipline builds a culture that saves hours of future conflict.

There will be times when someone tries to keep credit that is not theirs. Correct it calmly and in public spaces where the error was public. The benchmark came from Henry's prototype last quarter. Let us loop him for the next phase. No edge. No lecture. Only facts. If the pattern repeats, bring process to bear. Add a source line to slides by default. Add authors to documents with dates. Systems carry truth when memories get selective.

Do not forget to credit yourself. Self erasure is not noble. It confuses the record and it teaches people to overlook you. Use the same style you use for others. I led the synthesis and I would like to present the recommendations. Keep it simple. Keep it clean. Self credit lands well when you have a habit of lifting other names too.

Online, practice ethical credit. Link to the origin. Spell the name correctly. If you found a tool through a friend, include both the maker and the finder. This takes seconds and builds bridges you may walk later without knowing it yet.

If giving credit makes you worry about losing the spotlight, look at results over time. People who spread credit become nodes that others trust. Work flows toward them. They do not become smaller. The network makes them larger because they are known as a builder who tells the truth.

Try a small practice this week. At the end of each day, write three credits you can offer tomorrow. One at home. One at work. One in your wider circle. Keep them short and precise. Deliver them where they matter most. Email. Calendar invite. Team channel. Dinner table. Notice how the tone of your rooms changes when light is placed exactly where the work was done.

Credit is public kindness. It is also leadership. It turns a private virtue into a shared standard. When you make it normal, people stop fighting for attention and start building together. Say names. Say actions. Say impact. Let the truth travel farther than you do.

Law 32

Correct Without Humiliation

A well kept home fixes what is crooked without making a scene of the whole room. A napkin is straightened. A drip is wiped. The cake is turned gently so it bakes evenly. Correction in a kind life has the same touch. You fix the problem and keep the person whole. Shame breeds silence. Respect invites growth. The goal is not to score a point. The goal is to help tomorrow arrive smoother than today.

Begin with place and pace. Hard words land best in small rooms at a human speed. Move the talk away from an audience. Pour water. Sit so your knees face, not collide. Breathe once before you speak. A calm body gives your words a plate to sit on. Then keep the frame simple. I want a good result for both of us. Here is what happened. Here is what will help next time. Short, true, steady.

Name the act, not the identity. Say the dish was left in the sink, not you are lazy. Say the delivery missed Tuesday, not you are unreliable. People cannot change a label. They can change a behavior. When you point to the move rather than the person, you protect dignity while you protect standards.

Timing is part of kindness. Catch small misses early while they are light. You would not wait three weeks to wipe a spill. In the same way, a quiet note on day one spares a speech on day twenty. Two clean sentences can save a month of hurt feelings. When emotions run hot, take a short cooling minute. Touch the counter. Rinse your hands in warm water. Return when you can keep your voice gentle.

At home, correction is a lesson, not a verdict. A child knocks a glass. You hand them a towel and teach the motion that keeps the spill from spreading. Wipe from the seams toward the center. Then you practice setting the cup an inch from the edge. The child leaves with a skill and with their dignity intact. With partners, keep the pattern the same. Name the impact and the request without history's pile. When plans changed at the door, dinner fell apart on my side. Next time please text by four. I will do the same.

At work, keep feedback specific and useful. Put the moment, the effect, and the next step in one clear note. On Monday the report went out without the check. The client asked for a reissue. Add the noon cross check on Tuesdays and confirm in writing. If the team heard the miss, praise the repair in public later. Private correction, public credit. That rhythm grows adults rather than performers.

Language matters. Trade always and never for when and what. Trade blame for consequence that teaches. If you are late, the room waits and the work slips. Next week arrive five minutes early or message by nine. Keep your verbs strong and your adjectives few. Polite fog confuses. Sharp labels wound. Plain words in a warm tone do the real work.

Protect the less powerful. If someone is corrected harshly in front of others, redirect the tone with calm authority. We keep respect in this room. Let us pause and continue one at a time. Then invite the person back with care so they are not left standing alone under a bright light. A culture learns quickly what is safe. Make safety the rule.

Digital life requires extra restraint. Group threads are poor places for delicate fixes. Move the conversation to a smaller room or a short call. Put facts in order, name the effect, offer the next step, then stop. If a public correction is necessary, keep it brief and kind. You are modeling how to keep a community usable.

If you realize you humiliated someone, repair quickly and exactly. I corrected you in the wrong way. I am sorry. Here is what I meant to address, and here is what I admire about your work. Next time I will speak with you privately first. Then do it. People forgive more than you think when repair arrives cleanly and soon.

Your body can carry respect even when words are hard. Keep your face soft. Lower your shoulders. Rest your hands where they can be seen. Do not crowd. Let silence do a little lifting so the other person can absorb without defense. Offer water. Gentle rituals make tough truth feel survivable.

Teach this craft to children with small scripts. Try that again kindly. We pause when voices rise. We fix what we break together. Let them watch you accept correction without crumbling. Thank you. I missed that. I will update the note. A house where correction does not end love becomes a place where people risk doing brave things.

Build tiny supports that make kind correction easy to reach. Keep a note card near your desk with three lines. What happened. Why it mattered. What we try next. End family dinners with one simple appreciation so the room remembers that credit and care are the air we breathe. When praise is plentiful and specific, correction stops feeling like exile.

Do not confuse gentleness with softness on standards. You can insist on excellence without tearing fabric. Correction that is clear and kind tightens weave. It lets people bring their full effort without guarding their face. In that atmosphere teams improve, families relax, and friendships deepen because truth can live there.

Before you close this chapter, choose one relationship that could use a kinder way of correcting. Write a single sentence you can use the next time a small miss appears. Speak it in a warm tone and stop after the request. Notice how the room changes when shame is not invited to the table. It gets quieter. It gets braver. People look you in the eye.

Correct without humiliation. Fix the problem and keep the person whole. When you do, the work gets better, the bond grows stronger, and the house stays warm enough for growth.

That is the kind of leadership a gentle life requires.

Law 33

Be Specific, Then Be Brief

A beautiful table is not crowded. Each place setting has what it needs and nothing extra. Words can be set the same way. When you say exactly what you mean and stop, people relax. Vague praise confuses. Vague criticism wounds. Clarity is kindness, and brevity is respect for everyone's time.

Specificity starts with seeing. Notice the exact move that helped, then name it plainly. Instead of saying, "Great job," try, "You lowered your voice when the room heated up, and that kept us on track." The person now knows what to repeat. When something missed, keep the same precision. Trade "Do better" for "Please send the draft by noon with the figures checked against the sheet." The point is not to be sharp. The point is to be useful.

At home, give directions that a tired brain can follow. "Clean up" is fog. "Put the blue blocks in the bin, plates in the sink, then wash hands" is a path. With a partner, skip the speeches and place a small card on the counter. "Dinner at six. Text by four if plans change." The evening will taste softer because guessing has been removed from the recipe.

Your body helps your words land. Face the person. Lower your shoulders. Keep your hands where they can be seen. Speak in short lines with air between them. A calm posture makes concise language feel safe instead of stern. If you feel yourself rushing, take one sip of water and begin again with a single sentence.

At work, make specificity a house rule. Begin meetings with one sentence of purpose. End with owners and dates captured in writing. In messages, use a simple shape that fits on a recipe card: context, ask, deadline. "Client asked for a revised timeline. Please send the two line update by 3 pm." Skip "ASAP," which breeds anxiety. Time is kinder than speed.

Praise in public works best when it is precise. "Delivery was on time because Lila solved the vendor issue Tuesday morning." The room hears what mattered, and the person who did the work feels seen without a flare. When correction is needed, be just as exact and keep it private. "The report shipped without the noon cross check. Add it to Tuesdays and confirm in a note." The culture learns that truth is safe here.

Children bloom in this weather. When you like what you see, say the line that names it. "You put the books away and the room feels calm." When you want a change, give one step at a time. "Try that sentence again with a gentle voice." Small humans can carry small instructions. They also remember praise that fits like a well folded napkin.

Language tools help. Trade adjectives for verbs and numbers. Replace "soon" with "by 5." Replace "kind of messy" with "clear the counter and sink." Replace "keep me posted" with "send one sentence at noon and one at end of day." Specifics remove friction. Brevity removes clutter. Together they save everyone's patience for the real work.

Digital life loves extra, so you must love less. Write messages people can act on without scrolling. Put the ask at the top. Put supporting detail beneath. One link, not five. One paragraph, not a page. If a thread grows hot, move it to a smaller room and begin with a single clean line. "I want a good outcome for both of us. Here is what I see. Here is what I propose." Then stop and listen.

There is room for warmth inside precision. Begin with a soft opener and end with a thank you. "Morning, Maya. Please send the two slides by 10. Thank you." Courtesy is not decoration. It is the butter that helps clarity spread without tearing the bread.

When you miss and wander, repair quickly. "I gave you a speech. Here is the short version." Then give it. People forgive length when it comes with self correction. If someone else rambles, you can guide without sting. "This matters. Could you give me the one sentence version and the deadline you suggest." You are modeling the rules you want the house to keep.

Rituals make this easy to repeat. Keep a small card by your desk with three checks: Is it kind. Is it clear. Is it necessary. If a sentence fails one, tune it until it passes. In family life, set a nightly two minute huddle. Three specifics for tomorrow, then you are done. The whole home will feel lighter because the hallway is no longer clogged with vague plans.

Being brief does not mean being cold. It means serving the right portion. Being specific does not mean being harsh. It means feeding what works and pruning what does not. People cannot meet expectations they cannot see, and they cannot carry paragraphs when a sentence would do.

Before you close this chapter, choose one conversation that often tangles. Write the exact line you will use next time, one sentence that names the action and the time. Put it somewhere your hand can find it. When the moment arrives, set it on the table like a clean plate. Watch how faces soften when they understand you the first time.

Be specific, then be brief. Set the table, serve the meal, leave room for comfort. In that rhythm, kindness travels quickly and lands exactly where it is needed.

Law 34

Choose Curiosity Over Judgment

A kind home asks questions before it draws conclusions. It tastes the soup before adding salt. It checks the oven light before declaring the cake a failure. Curiosity is that gentle habit of looking closer. Judgment slams a lid on the pot and calls it done. When you choose curiosity, you keep heat low and flavors true. You make room for truth to finish cooking.

Judgment is fast. It loves shortcuts. It decides a tone meant disrespect when it might have meant fatigue. It declares a child rude when the shoes were too tight. It writes a story about a late reply when the person was caring for a parent. Curiosity moves slower. It asks what else could be true. It turns on a lamp, sets a glass of water on the table, and invites context to sit down.

Begin with your body. Judgment tightens the jaw and narrows the eyes. Curiosity softens the face and opens the chest. Put both feet on the floor. Touch the counter with all ten fingertips.

Breathe in for a slow count of five and out for five. Ask one quiet question inside your own head. What am I missing. Your voice will come out kinder after that small reset.

At home, curiosity changes evenings. When a partner arrives short on words, judgment wants to label it cold. Curiosity tries, You look drained. Do you want quiet or company. When a child spills after a long day, judgment says you always do this. Curiosity says, Tell me what happened right before the cup tipped. Then you learn the stool wobbled and the floor gets a felt pad. The house improves because the real cause was found.

In friendship, curiosity protects the bond. A friend cancels twice. Judgment writes a script about priorities. Curiosity asks, Is something heavy on your side. Do we need a different rhythm. You may learn the schedule needs a morning walk instead of late dinners. Small changes become possible when you stop defending your first theory.

Work thrives on this law. A teammate misses a mark. Judgment holds a meeting that sounds like a verdict. Curiosity invites facts. Walk me through your week from Monday morning. Often you will discover a blocked input, a hidden dependency, or a simple misunderstanding about ownership. Then you can place one clear fix instead of three new rules that only add noise.

Language carries curiosity when you choose it. Try lines that open doors. Help me understand how you arrived there. What would a good outcome look like on Friday. What did I miss on my side. When feelings run bright, keep words short. I want this to go well for both of us. Tell me the part that matters most to you. People relax when they hear questions that are safe to answer.

Curiosity needs boundaries to stay generous. It is not an invitation to endure harm. If disrespect arrives, place your line first. I want a good conversation. I will continue when the tone is respectful. When safety is restored, become curious again. What set us off. What would help next time. In this way, curiosity and standards live in the same house.

With children, make a game of noticing before naming. You seem fidgety. Are your socks scratchy or is your brain tired. Would you like to switch chairs or take a water break. Small people learn to scan their own state when you model it. Later they will bring that skill to school and work, which saves everyone energy.

Your inner talk matters too. Judgment toward yourself can feel like efficiency, but it makes slow learners out of all of us. Replace Why did I mess this up with What step was missing from my setup. Replace I am terrible at this with I have not learned the sequence yet. Then add the missing step to a card and tape it where your hands will see it. Curiosity turns shame into method.

Digital life rewards judgment because it is quick and loud. Choose to be slow and precise. Ask for a source. Read beyond a headline. If a post stings, let it cool before you reply. Move heated topics out of crowded rooms. When you must correct, keep it factual and short. If you are wrong, say so quickly. Curiosity keeps communities usable.

There is a rhythm that makes curiosity practical. Notice, name, and nudge. Notice what you observed without heat. Name the question that matters. Nudge the next clear step. I noticed the delivery slipped by two hours. What blocked it. Let us add a noon check on Tuesdays. This rhythm keeps dignity intact while the work gets better.

Rituals help. Keep a card by the sink that reads Three Curious Questions. What else could be true. What matters most here. What is the smallest next step. Touch it before tough talks. Begin meetings with one minute of quiet reading so people can gather facts before reacting. End with owners and dates so curiosity does not become drift.

If you catch yourself judging, repair in the moment. I jumped to a conclusion. I am sorry. Tell me again. People forgive a quick reset. They grow wary of a person who never adjusts. Curiosity is a skill, not a personality trait. Practice makes it natural.

Protect your energy while you practice. Curiosity can be tiring if you give it to every noise at the door. Offer it to what you are responsible for and to who you love. For strangers in loud spaces, keep your standards simple. I will engage where facts and respect are present. I will step away where they are not. Your peace is part of the project.

Before you close this chapter, try a small exercise. Think of a recent irritation. Write your first judgment in one sentence. Then write three alternate stories that could also be true. Choose one kind question you will ask next time instead of delivering the verdict. Keep it on a small card in your pocket.

Use it once this week and watch how the air changes.

Choose curiosity over judgment. Taste before you season. Ask before you decide. When you do, you save relationships from avoidable bruises, you discover fixes that work, and you turn your rooms into places where truth feels safe to speak. That is how kindness keeps its flavor and its strength.

Law 35

Keep Confidences Like a Vault

Trust is built in quiet. People place pieces of their lives in your hands and wait to see what you do next. When you keep a confidence, you tell the world who you are. You say my word is safe, my rooms are safe, my presence is a door that closes softly. That safety is kindness in its most durable form.

A vault has three qualities. It is selective about what enters. It holds firmly what it keeps. It opens only with permission or for true safety. Treat confidences the same way. Do not collect what you do not need. Guard what you agree to hold. Share only with clear consent or when life and law require protection.

Begin with clarity at the moment of sharing. When someone says do not tell anyone, slow the scene. Ask a clean question so both of you understand the promise. Do you want this private between us, or may I ask one trusted person for advice without names. Do you need me to act, or do you only need a listener. These simple lines prevent confusion and keep you from carrying a burden you cannot lift.

Your body is part of the vault. Sit steady. Keep your eyes warm. Let your phone rest face down. Do not rush to fill silence. People speak more honestly when they sense they will not be managed or exposed. When they finish, reflect the shape of what you heard in a few calm sentences. I hear how heavy this is. Here is what I understand. Here is what I can hold. Here is what I cannot hold. Now the edges are visible and trust has room to breathe.

Confidentiality has boundaries. If someone is in danger, if a child is at risk, or if a crime is present, you are responsible to act. Say so with care and with respect. I love you and I cannot keep this to myself. I will help you find the right help now. Then follow through. Confidentiality that protects harm is not kindness. It is neglect dressed as loyalty. True loyalty seeks safety and repair.

At home, set privacy as a house rule. Do not read what is not addressed to you. Do not use a story from one child to entertain another. Do not turn a partner's hard moment into a group joke. If family news must be shared, ask for consent and timing. May I tell my sister by tomorrow. I will keep it short. Your people will relax near you because they know their messy middle will not become a tale at dinner.

In friendship, guard the unseen work. If a friend confides about debt, illness, fear, or a new start, do not build your identity as the caring one on their private information. Be present, help with tasks, and keep the story off stage. If you slip and tell someone, repair quickly. Name the breach, own the harm, say what you will do to limit the spread, and ask what they need now. Then live your promise. Repair cannot erase a leak, but it can stop further loss.

At work, practice minimum necessary sharing. Use only the names and details that the task requires. Move sensitive topics to smaller rooms with clear notes and limited access. Label documents that contain private information and store them where only the right people can reach them. Speak in facts rather than gossip when you must discuss an issue. The goal is a decision that protects both people and standards, not a storyline.

Digital life needs care. Group chats feel like living rooms, but they are archives. Screenshots travel. Before you type a private detail, stop and ask whether you would want to see that sentence outside the circle. If you would not, do not send it. If you must keep notes for a serious matter, keep them factual, brief, and secure. Consider how long they should exist. Confidences deserve a life cycle, not an endless shelf.

Language helps you hold the vault shut without sounding cold. Try lines like these. Thank you for trusting me. I will keep this private. I need to think for an hour before I respond so I speak with care. I cannot hold this alone. May I ask a counselor or an elder for guidance without sharing your name. I will not discuss this outside the plan we agree to. The tone is steady and humane. The commitment is real.

There is a difference between privacy and secrecy. Privacy

protects dignity and gives people space to grow. Secrecy hides patterns that cause harm. Ask yourself what the information does in the world. If it keeps someone safe or gives them time, keep it private. If it covers a cycle of abuse or deceit, move it toward light with the correct help. You are not a vault for harm. You are a vault for healing.

Teach this law to children by modeling it. When they share, do not rush to retell. If you need to involve another adult, explain why and how. I want you safe, and I will talk to the school counselor with you tomorrow. When you keep their small confidences, they will bring you the big ones before they break.

Guard against the soft leak. It sounds like I cannot say who or I heard something I probably should not say and then a breadcrumb appears. Soft leaks are still leaks. They train you to use other people's lives as entertainment. Replace the habit with blessings and boundaries. Wish people well in silence. Change the subject. Offer a next step that does not require more details. Your rooms will grow kinder as gossip starves.

Your own heart needs a vault as well. Keep a private journal that is not a report to the world. Store your raw drafts there. Do not expose every emotion to every feed. When you have processed, you can choose public truth with dignity. A person who guards their inner life becomes a person whose outer word carries weight.

If a confidence becomes too heavy, seek permission to share a small piece for support. I am feeling stretched and want to get wise counsel. May I ask one neutral person for help without names or specifics. If permission is refused and the weight is unmanageable, set a limit with care. I love you and I cannot keep this level of detail. I can still help with rides and meals. Kindness includes protecting your capacity so you do not break.

Close with a simple practice. For seven days, treat every story that is not yours as if it were held behind a gentle door. Before you tell it, ask whose trust it belongs to, what purpose sharing would serve, and whether you have consent. If the answers do not honor dignity, keep the door shut. Each time you do, you strengthen a muscle people can feel. They will come to you not because you know everything, but because you do not sell what you know.

Keep confidences like a vault. Take in carefully. Hold with honor. Open only for safety or with permission. A life lived this way becomes a refuge. In that refuge, kindness multiplies, truth feels safe to speak, and your name becomes a quiet promise that other people can rely on.

Law 36

Exit Clean

Exiting clean is the art of leaving without smoke. It is not ghosting and it is not a performance. It is simple stewardship. You close the loop, you return what is not yours, you speak one kind truth, and you walk. Leaving this way protects your dignity and the dignity of the room you are leaving. It also protects your future. People remember how you depart.

A clean exit starts with clarity. Ask yourself three quiet questions. What promise did I make. What impact will my leaving have. What can I do today to reduce friction for those who stay. Answer in plain sentences, then act. Cancel what should be cancelled. Hand off what must continue. Name what will stop.

At home, a clean exit looks small and steady. You put the dish in the rack before you go. You tell a child when you will be back and who is in charge while you are gone. You say I am stepping outside to breathe and I will return in ten minutes. You do not slam the door. You do not leave people guessing.

With a partner, clean exits keep hard moments from turning into damage. If a talk is too hot, you pause with respect rather than storm out. Say I care about this. I am not calm enough to continue. I will return at seven to finish. Then keep the time. When a relationship must end, you state the truth without cruelty. I am not the right partner for you and I am grateful for what we shared. Here is how I will return your things. Here is how we can handle the next thirty days. Your tone stays warm while your plan stays firm.

In friendship, a clean exit honors history. Not every season lasts. When the pattern wears you down, do not disappear without a word. Write a short note that names the truth without blame. I do not have the capacity to keep this level of contact. I am stepping back. I wish you well. You may not get applause. That is not the aim. The aim is to stop leaking hurt by half leaving for months.

At work, exiting clean is professional kindness. Give adequate notice. Offer a brief, factual transition doc. List projects, current status, owners, dates, and links. Share passwords through the proper secure channel. Credit people in writing so their work does not evaporate when you leave the room. If you are a manager, meet one on one with each direct report. Say what will change and what will not. Do not use your exit to settle scores. Your receipts are clarity, not spectacle.

Clean exits include returning what you borrowed. Tools, books, contacts, trust. If you used a colleague's template, leave your improved version for the team. If you took emotional room with a long vent, give back order by sending the summary or doing the task you avoided. If you borrowed a platform, thank the host in public and point future opportunities their way. Return what you take, then close the door gently behind you.

Language is your ally. Keep a few lines ready that sound like you. Thank you for the time we shared. Here is what I can commit to during transition. Here is what I am unable to continue. I wish you well and I am stepping away. I will not discuss details beyond this note. Short sentences prevent long arguments. They also keep you from speaking from heat.

Your body helps you leave well. Before you announce an exit, settle your pace. Inhale for four counts, hold for two, exhale for six. Drop your shoulders one inch. This will soften your face and lower your voice. People hear a steady voice even when the message is sad. You are less likely to over share when your breath is calm.

Digital life needs its own clean exit. Archive shared folders you own. Remove access you no longer should hold. Set a clear away message with a date and a handoff contact. Close threads with a final short reply that links to the place where decisions now live. Do not leave small fires in group chats and expect others to put them out. End with facts, not a speech.

Sometimes an exit requires consequence. If a room refuses respect, you can end the meeting and name why. If an online exchange turns cruel, you can block and move on. Exiting clean does not mean you accept harm. It means you choose a boundary that does not add extra harm on the way out.

LAW 36

Repair belongs inside this law. If you contributed to the mess, say so in one sentence and add one act. I missed two deadlines. I have documented the process so you are not left guessing. Then stop. A clean exit does not turn into a long confession. It offers enough truth to honor people's time and then it releases the scene.

Expect feelings. Leaving well does not remove grief, anger, or relief. It removes confusion. That is your part. The rest belongs to time. When doubt rises after you exit, return to your answers. I kept my word. I reduced friction. I spoke with respect. Let that be enough.

Measure results by the quiet that follows. A clean exit lowers drama and raises order. People know what to do next. You sleep without writing speeches in your head. Your name stays light. Doors you may need later do not slam because you did not slam them first.

Practice this law on a small scale today. Choose one place to exit clean. End a conversation you cannot hold with a warm boundary. Close a project with a two paragraph summary. Return a borrowed item with a thank you. Wish someone well in private and release a thread you keep checking. Feel the air clear as you do.

Exit clean. Close loops. Return what is not yours. Speak one kind truth. Walk with a steady back. The future will be easier to enter because you left the past in order.

Law 37

Apologize Like It Matters

A real apology is an act of repair. It is not a performance, not a way to make discomfort disappear, and not a charm you wave so consequences vanish. A real apology names the harm, owns the choice, asks what repair looks like, and then does the work. When you apologize like it matters, you turn a mistake into a bridge instead of a wall.

Begin with four plain sentences. I did this. It affected you like this. I am sorry. Here is what I will do next. Speak them without decoration. Do not add a paragraph of reasons. Reasons can live later, after the wound is acknowledged and a plan is in motion. If your mouth reaches for if or but, stop. Those two words turn an apology into self defense.

Your body tells the truth about your apology. Settle your breath. Lower your shoulders one inch. Keep your voice steady and calm. Look at the person without staring them down. This posture says I am here to take responsibility, not to barter my

LAW 37

way out of it. People hear sincerity in a regulated voice more than in eloquent phrases.

Apologize for your action, not for their feelings. Say I missed the deadline and that put you in a hard spot, not I am sorry you feel upset. Feelings matter, but they are the echo. Name the strike and the impact. Then ask a clean question. Did I get that right. Listen to the answer. Let them add what you missed. You are not losing power when you listen. You are aligning facts so repair can be precise.

At home, apologize quickly and specifically. You raised your voice at a child. Kneel to their level. I was loud. That was not respectful. I scared you. I am sorry. I will speak quietly and take a breath before I answer. Then show the change the next time you are tested. Children trust apologies that come with proof.

With a partner, timing matters. If heat is still high, start with a short acknowledgment and a plan to return. I was hurt and I also crossed a line. I need a walk. At seven I will apologize and talk about repair. Then keep the time and keep the promise. When you return, state your part without asking for immediate forgiveness. You are responsible for repair. They are responsible for their yes, their no, or their not yet.

At work, match the scale of the apology to the scale of the miss. Private mistake, private apology. Public mistake, public repair. If a wrong call cost the team time, write a brief note that names what happened, the impact, and the correction. I chose X. It delayed Y. We are shifting to Z and I will send a checkpoint Friday. Then meet the checkpoint exactly. A clean written repair protects the team from gossip and keeps work moving.

An apology does not cancel consequence. If trust was damaged, access may change while you rebuild. Accept that without drama. This is part of making things right. Offer a plan with dates and guardrails. Invite verification. I will send weekly updates for the next month. If I miss one, move the decision to someone else. Consequence paired with willingness builds real confidence faster than pretty words.

Beware of over apologizing. Constant sorry does not create safety. It creates fog. If you did nothing wrong, use gratitude and clarity instead. Thank you for waiting. Thank you for the feedback. Here is what I can do. Save the word sorry for the moments it deserves. Then let it carry weight.

Language helps. Keep a small script ready so you do not improvise from panic.
 I did X.
 It affected you by Y.
 I am sorry.
 Here is my repair.
 Did I miss anything important.
 Say it once, slowly. If the other person wants to talk, listen. If they insult or escalate, keep your boundary and offer to resume when both of you can speak with respect.

Repair requires action. Replace the broken item. Return the money. Rework the file. Meet the new date. Change the system that made the mistake likely. Apology is the door. Repair is you walking through it with tools. Without repair, the door leads back to the same room.

There will be harms that cannot be fixed fully. You cannot return time lost in sickness or ease lost after betrayal. Name the limits honestly and still offer what reduces future harm. We cannot undo this. I can pay the fee and document the process so it will not happen again. Honest limits feel kinder than false promises.

Your nervous system needs care after a hard apology. Drink water. Step outside. Write a simple note to yourself that names what you learned and what you will do next. Shame wants to make a forever story out of a single mistake. Do not let it. Hold yourself accountable and also let yourself grow.

Model this law for children and teams. Let them see you apologize without groveling. Let them hear you say I am sorry, and here is the plan. They will learn that strength and remorse can live in the same person. They will also learn that repair is a craft, not a mood.

Online, apologize with the same clarity. Correct the post. Pin the correction. Name the source you missed. Do not argue with people who want a show. Put your attention on the fix and then step away. Your goal is to reduce harm and raise accuracy, not to win a comment thread.

Close with a small practice for the week. Think of a place where your apology is due. Write four lines. Action. Impact. Sorry. Repair. Read them out loud once. Deliver them in a steady voice. Then do the repair within the time you named. At the end of the week, ask yourself two questions. Did trust move, even a little.

Did I change the condition that created the harm. Adjust until both answers become yes.

Apologize like it matters. Name the harm. Own it. Repair it. Then live the change. When you do, you turn an injury into new strength and you become a person whose word can carry weight again.

Law 38

Starve Gossip

A kind house does not serve meals made of other people. It serves soup, bread, and stories that the teller owns. When talk turns toward the absent, a good host lowers the flame. If they are not here, we keep it factual or we keep it quiet. Protect the absent and you protect your own name.

Gossip pretends to be intimacy. It arrives with flavor, asks you to lean in, and promises a feeling of being on the inside. The taste is quick and the aftertaste is bitter. Your spirit knows the difference between warmth and heat. Warmth leaves the room softer. Heat leaves the room noisy and sticky. Choose warmth. Let the dish of unasked stories go cold.

You can hear the shift when gossip starts. The voice moves from sharing to sharpening. A pause becomes an opening to add a little spice that no one asked for. In that moment, starve the story with a gentle choice. Change the subject to something present and useful. Offer praise that balances the air. Move the talk to a room where help can happen, not harm. Small moves save evenings.

At home, set a simple rule that everyone can remember. If a person is not in the room, we speak with the same respect we would use to their face. If the topic is tender, we ask permission before we share. Children learn this faster than adults because they still feel tone with their whole bodies. Praise them when they keep a sibling's privacy. Thank them when they correct themselves. The house becomes a place where trust rises like bread.

With partners and friends, be brave enough to keep boundaries. If a conversation slides toward someone else's mistakes, place a clean line without a lecture. I want us to keep our talk hopeful. Can we focus on what we can do. Then bring up work that belongs to you. What can we change this week. Where can we offer help. Curiosity about solutions feeds connection. Curiosity about another person's private life feeds nothing good.

Workplace culture lives on what is repeated. Choose to repeat what builds. Credit names with care. Risks are shared with owners, not with spectators. If a colleague tries to hand you a story that stains, be the steady counter. I do not have context. Let us ask them directly. If you must discuss a problem in someone's absence, stick to facts and plans. The invoice is late. I will email the owner and copy you. We will revisit on Thursday. You have turned a rumor into a task.

Digital life multiplies the cost of loose talk. Screens invite performance and speed. Choose friction. Do not forward private messages into group rooms. Do not post a screenshot of what someone trusted you to hold. If you made a mistake and shared too far, repair in the same corridor where you spilled. Delete what you can. Apologize to the person you exposed. Tell the group that the thread is closing. Your steadiness will be remembered more than your stumble.

Gossip feeds on adrenaline. Your body can remove the fuel. Lower your shoulders. Unclench your jaw. Drink water. Pause before answering a question that invites you to judge. A calm body makes it easier to say the sentence that saves the room. That is not my story to tell. Let me help you reach them. Then change the topic to the weather of the day. The weather has rescued more friendships than we admit.

There are exceptions that prove the rule. Silence is not kindness when harm is present. If someone is unsafe, you speak to the right person, clearly and soon. You do it in a room that can help, not a room that enjoys the story. That is not gossip. That is care with a backbone.

When you have gossiped, repair matters. Admit what you did without fog. I told a story that was not mine. I am sorry. Here is who heard it. I have asked them not to pass it further. Then keep the new line exactly. People forgive a miss faster than they forgive the person who refuses to stop.

Rituals help starve gossip before it sits down. Begin dinners with one good thing someone in the room did today so praise is the first flavor. End meetings with one sentence of public credit so people leave full of the names that deserve light. When a circle feels thin, serve a task. Fold napkins. Wash fruit. Walk around the block. Hands that are busy have less room for idle harm.

Language is your set of utensils. Keep a few ready. That belongs to them. Let us give them space to tell it. I want to keep the room kind. What is the next useful step. These lines are short, steady, and easy to reach. Use them until they feel like muscle memory.

Think about what gossip costs you. It weakens your name. It trains your mind to look for flaws rather than for ways to help. It steals time from the work and the rest that would actually improve your life. You deserve better use of your attention. The people you love deserve the same.

Before you close this chapter, try a small fast. Choose one place where gossip tends to appear. A chat thread, a break room table, a porch after dinner. For seven days, bring only respect and useful facts to that place. If the talk turns sharp, set your line and offer a new path. If you cannot improve the room, leave it quietly. At the end of the week, notice how your chest feels. Lighter. Cleaner. Ready for better talk.

Starve gossip. Feed what is present. Feed what is useful. Feed what is yours to carry. When you keep that diet, your rooms become safe places to show up as you are. Trust grows. Work improves. Even silence feels friendly. That is the taste of a house that refuses to dine on missing people.

Law 39

Build Rooms Where Others Can Win

Winning is not luck in a good room. It is design. A room that lets people win has clear aims, fair rules, visible paths to credit, and tools that reduce friction. It makes skill louder than status. It turns help into a system rather than a favor. When you build rooms like this, kindness becomes structure. People relax. Work improves. Trust grows.

Start with the aim. A room without a purpose becomes a stage. Write the purpose in one sentence where all can see it. Here is the decision we need. Here is the draft we will improve. Here is the plan we will leave with. A clear aim keeps loud voices from taking the day. It also lets quiet skill find its lane.

Set simple rules that protect dignity. Begin on time. End on time. One person speaks at once. Phones away unless needed for the task. If someone is interrupted, they finish. If voices rise, you pause. Rules are not mood. They are guardrails so ideas can move.

Design for access. Make it easy to prepare and easy to contribute. Share materials early. Use agendas. Label who will speak and for how long. Rotate roles. Let a junior teammate run the next review. Invite the person who owns the detail to answer the detail. Use captions on calls. Choose rooms with light, chairs that fit, and air that is quiet. Small design choices tell a nervous system that it is safe to try.

Credit is part of the room. Say names when you win. Put contributors at the top of notes. Tag the source on the slide. Ask, Who should be in this room for their work to be seen. Sponsorship belongs here too. Offer the stage and stay nearby. You are not only opening a door. You are standing there long enough to make sure it closes behind both of you without catching a hand.

Build tools that remove friction. Checklists. Decision logs. Templates for updates. Shared calendars that are accurate. A short form that collects what a reviewer needs the first time. Tools prevent beginners from being blamed for system gaps. Tools also free experts to do deep work rather than answer the same question all week.

Make feedback teach. Correct without humiliation. Be specific. Here is what missed. Here is one model to follow. Here is the next small step and the date. Invite questions. Keep tone steady. Repair quickly when you misstep. The room learns that truth and kindness can sit at the same table.

At home, build rooms for winning in simple ways. Lower shelves so children can put things away without help. Place a stool by the sink. Use picture labels for bins. Post the morning routine in five lines. The goal is not control. The goal is to let people succeed without needing you to translate the world every time.

With a partner, make winning mutual. Share the map for the week. Who is on pickups. Who cooks. Who rests. Who resets the house on Saturday. Agree on a budget for time and money. Use a shared list. The point is not to track each other. The point is to remove surprise. Surprises drain goodwill. Maps protect it.

Online, build rooms that do not eat people. Moderate clearly. Pin rules. Remove cruelty fast and in writing. Credit makers. Link sources. Close old threads with a summary. Surface useful answers so new people do not have to dig. The internet can be a hard room. Structure makes it gentler.

Mind the clock. Time zones. Caregiving hours. Commutes. Schedule big moments when the most people can join. Record when you can. Share decisions in writing. Do not punish someone for living a life while they also work. A fair clock is a quiet form of love.

Pronounce names correctly. Ask once. Practice. Write the phonetic note if needed. Use people's titles and pronouns as they choose them. This is not decor. It is entry. A person who hears their name with care will bring better work and more truth.

Your body helps you build rooms. Sit with a calm back and

warm eyes. Breathe low. Speak at a pace that fits thought. Turn your shoulders toward the next speaker. These cues lower threat. They also tell the room that you are here to host, not to dominate.

Language matters. Keep a few lines ready. What would help you win here. What decision do we need today. Who else should be in this room. What is the smallest next step. Let us write that so no one has to remember. Thank you, this part was yours. These sentences move attention to the work and to the person doing it.

Do not confuse building with rescuing. A good room asks for effort. It does not remove all struggle. It removes unfair struggle. Let people carry their share. Give them tools, time, and a clear target. Then get out of the way. Growth needs room to move.

Hold boundaries. If someone refuses the rules, pause them. If someone takes over, redirect gently. I want to hear three voices we have not heard. If patterns persist, change roles or access. A kind room still has doors. You are allowed to close one to protect the many.

Measure what matters. Track outcomes, not airtime. Track how often new voices lead. Track how many decisions stick without rework. Track how people sleep. A good room reduces late night panic. It increases clear mornings. If the numbers do not move, change the design. Ask for feedback in one page. Then test a new rule for a week.

LAW 39

Teach this law by making wins visible. Celebrate small firsts. First pull request. First client call. First talk given. Tie praise to effort and to the system that made it possible. Your practice will outlive you when you show others how to host.

Close with a simple practice. Pick one room you run this week. Write a one sentence aim. Set three rules. Name one voice you will bring forward. Prepare one tool that reduces friction. Decide how you will give credit. After the room ends, send a six line note. Aim. Decision. Owners. Date. Thanks. Next step. Do this three times. Watch the room get kinder and stronger.

Build rooms where others can win. Set the aim. Protect the rules. Share the stage. Remove the sand from the gears. Give credit like sunlight. People will grow inside what you design. And you will be known as the person whose rooms make good things possible.

Law 40

Curate Your Circle

Kindness is contagious and so is chaos. The people nearest to you set your pace, shape your standards, and influence your peace. Curating your circle is not about status. It is about stewardship. You choose who has regular access to your time, your mind, and your home. You do this with a warm heart and a clear eye so your life can hold the weight you carry.

Start with a simple truth. Proximity writes habits. Spend your days around people who prize honesty, repair, and follow through and you will practice those things without trying. Spend your days around people who feed drama and dodge accountability and you will spend your energy cleaning messes that are not yours. Your circle is a greenhouse. Decide what you want to grow and plant accordingly.

Begin by noticing how you feel after time with someone. Your body will tell you the truth before your mind writes a story. Do you feel easier to breathe. Do you feel steady and a little braver.

Or do you feel small, tight, and tired. Do you need to rehearse what you said. Pay attention to these signals. Kindness can be generous with the world and still selective with daily access.

Healthy circles share a few qualities. Truth is welcome. Boundaries are respected. Repair is normal. Credit travels. Joy shows up in ordinary ways. People celebrate wins without turning them into competition. People name misses without turning them into humiliation. When a mistake happens, there is a path back that includes accountability and support. You can be fully yourself and still be called higher.

Curating does not mean cutting people with a hard edge. It means placing relationships at the distance that protects dignity for both sides. Some belong in the inner room. Some belong on the porch. Some belong outside the gate with a blessing from afar. The distance can change over time. Seasons shift. People grow. What matters is that you choose the distance on purpose rather than letting habit decide for you.

At home, curate with rhythms that keep the house calm. Choose a few families that share similar values and make regular time with them. Keep gatherings simple so they can repeat. Eat together. Walk together. Trade small kindnesses that lift the week. You are not building a club. You are building a support system that keeps children and adults surrounded by steady examples.

With a partner, curate as a team. Share a short list of people who pour into the bond and a short list of people who pull it thin. Decide together how much access each group gets and what guardrails keep the partnership healthy. A strong couple protects the calendar with care. Yes to the friend who makes both of you better. Less to the friend who uses your home as a stage for conflict.

At work, curate by choosing collaborators who honor the standard. Seek people who tell the truth early, write decisions, and return what they borrow. Say yes to those who think about the whole system rather than only their lane. You will still work with all kinds of people. The circle you invite into your closest projects should be the ones who keep both quality and tone intact under pressure.

Curating includes your digital life. Unfollow accounts that feed envy or outrage. Follow makers who share tools, context, and hope. Mute threads that bring you into arguments you did not choose. Build small group chats where generosity and accuracy are the norm. Your phone is a gate. Set it so the garden inside you can grow.

Set clear entry rules for the inner circle. They can be quiet rules that you hold privately. Tell the truth. Keep confidences. Apologize when wrong. Celebrate without keeping score. Protect time. If someone repeatedly refuses these basics, reduce access. You can love them and still keep them at a distance that does not cost your health.

Language helps you curate without cruelty. Keep a few lines ready. Thank you for thinking of me. I am keeping my calendar very simple this season. I am not available for late night calls. I respond during the day. I want to stay in good shape for my family and my work. I care about you and I am stepping back for a while. Speak these sentences once or twice. Then let your calendar reflect them.

There will be guilt. Many of us were taught that kindness means constant availability. Replace that measure with a better one. Kindness keeps dignity intact, yours included. If a connection repeatedly collapses your peace, it does not belong in your daily circle. Bless it. Release it. Put your energy where it builds life.

Curating is not about finding perfect people. It is about choosing teachable people. The best circles are not free of conflict. They are skilled at repair. They ask clean questions. They disagree with respect. They keep the aim in view. They tell you when you have spinach in your teeth and they cheer when you speak on stage. Aim for that mix. Depth and honesty. Lightness and fun.

Your circle also needs elders and beginners. Elders are the ones ahead of you in life or craft. They save you years by telling the truth about what lasts. Beginners keep you curious. They see options you no longer notice. Make room for both. Take a walk with an auntie who tells you how she stayed married through hard years. Take coffee with a new teammate who sees the product from a fresh angle. Wisdom and novelty belong together.

Guard your capacity. Even the best circle needs space between gatherings. Keep quiet windows. Protect sleep. Say no early when your week is full. Your presence is most generous when it is not stretched thin. People who love you will respect the shape you need in order to keep showing up with a whole heart.

If someone in your circle begins to harm others or to harm you, act with clarity. Speak once about what you see. Name the boundary and the consequence. If the pattern continues, step away. Do this without a speech or a smear. You are not a judge. You are a gardener. You remove what chokes the roots so the rest can thrive.

Use a short audit each month. Write three names that give you strength. Write three that drain you. Add one step for each column. Invite the first group closer with a call, a note, or a simple plan. Add a boundary for the second group or move them to a distance that fits your health. Small adjustments compound. Your days will feel different because your rooms will feel different.

Teach this law to children and teams by modeling it. Let them see you choose friends who treat others well. Let them hear you decline invitations that would make you thin and sharp. Let them watch you apologize when you are wrong and keep people who do the same. They will learn that community is a practice, not an accident.

Close with a gentle practice for this week. Choose one person who makes you braver and schedule an hour together. Choose one person who leaves you tense and set a kind boundary for the next thirty days. Then notice your sleep, your tone, and your focus. Curating your circle is not cold. It is careful. It keeps your heart soft and your life strong. When your circle honors truth, timing, and peace, kindness has a home to live in.

Law 41

Plant For A Future You Will Not See

Kindness gets stronger when it stretches beyond your timeline. Planting for a future you will not see is a decision to invest in people, places, and systems that may never say your name. It is humility turned into design. It is love with a calendar.

Planting begins with a shift in measure. Ask not only what helps today. Ask what will still help in five years. Ask what will reduce confusion when you are not in the room. Ask what will make a child, a neighbor, or a teammate's life gentler long after this moment passes. When you think this way, your choices change shape. You move from clever fixes to steady foundations.

At home, plant in ordinary soil. Teach skills that free people rather than keeping them dependent. Show a child how to make a grocery list and stretch a budget. Label a shelf so a partner does not have to ask where things live. Write down favorite recipes in simple steps. These are small seeds. They grow into confidence and ease. They reduce future friction. They also say

I want you strong even when I am not near.

With a partner, plant by building rhythms that can survive stress. Keep a shared calendar accurate. Choose a weekly money check in that is short and calm. Agree on a rule for conflict that protects both of you. We pause when voices rise. We return at seven. These habits look plain. They carry you through hard seasons because the scaffolding already exists.

With friends, plant by making introductions that will outlast you. When you connect two people who should know each other, add context and step back. Give enough light so the new tie can grow without you. If you benefit from a community, offer to maintain the map, the document, or the welcome message for the next person. Community endures when someone tends the path.

At work, planting looks like documentation, cross training, and clean systems. Write decisions in one place where new teammates can find them. Create a short checklist that prevents repeat errors. Share the simple template that cut your time in half. Teach your craft to someone younger without keeping a secret step. A team that plants knowledge will not collapse when one person changes roles. That is kindness to people and to the mission.

Money can plant too. Pay on time. Support a local shop you want your neighborhood to keep. Give small and regular rather than large and rare if that makes your giving reliable. If you profit from a culture or a source, send some of that profit back to keep the well from drying. Planting with money says the circle matters more than one moment of gain.

Plant in the ground you stand on. Care for a patch of soil or a pot on a windowsill. Children remember the day you placed a seed in dirt and checked it each morning. Teach them to water without flooding. Teach them to wait. A seed's pace is a lesson in patience and faithfulness that no lecture can replace.

Digital life needs planting as well. The internet forgets easily. Help it remember the right things. Write guides. Tag sources. Archive the best answers and pin them where new people will look first. If you run a space online, set clear rules and hand off the keys when you rest. A good room should live after the host takes a nap.

Language supports long horizons. Keep a few lines that point beyond yourself. I may not see the results, and I will do my part today. I am building this for the person who will sit here next. Thank you to the people who started this before me. When you talk this way you lower ego and raise continuity. People lean in because they can feel the work is bigger than any one pair of hands.

Planting requires boundaries. You cannot water every field. Choose a few places and go deep. Protect quiet windows so you can plan rather than react. Say no to the urgent that steals from the important. Say yes to the slow build even when no one claps. This is how roots reach water.

Your body will help you keep the pace. Long work wants a steady nervous system. Breathe in for four, hold for two, and out for six before big choices. Move your shoulders down one inch. Drink water. Sleep. You will think farther into the future when your body is not running on fumes.

Credit is part of planting. Say names of those who planted before you. Tell their stories at the table and in the meeting. Include them in the document where decisions are recorded. When people see a lineage, they understand they are part of a living thing. They feel responsible to leave it better than they found it.

Do not confuse planting with control. Seeds are not scripts. You prepare the ground, you place what you can, you tend, you release. Students will surpass you. Children will do it their way. Teams will refine your checklist. This is success. Planting aims at fruit, not at fame.

There will be days when planting feels small. A label on a drawer. A sentence in a handbook. A twenty minute lesson. Trust compound interest. Trust the math of gentle repetition. One clear note prevents ten future questions. One calm practice saves a hundred future apologies. That is quiet power.

If grief rises because you will not see the finished tree, honor it. Then look for the sprouts that do appear. The neighbor using your bench. The teammate teaching someone with the document you wrote. The child washing an apple without being asked. These are postcards from the future. Keep going.

Close with a simple practice for this week. Pick one room you touch often. Home, work, community, online. Ask three questions. What confuses people here. What breaks when I am gone. What would help the next person win. Create one small thing that answers those questions. A label. A checklist. A short welcome note. Share it and step back. You just planted.

Plant for a future you will not see. Teach, document, introduce, repair, and tend. Let your kindness travel past your lifetime and your calendar. The world will not always know your name for it. It will feel the shade.

Law 42

Let Grace Be The Last Move

Grace is the choice to end with dignity after truth, boundary, and consequence have done their work. It is not pretending nothing happened. It is not letting harm continue. Grace is the closing note that says I will not carry this forward as poison. I will carry it forward as wisdom. When grace is the last move, you protect your spirit and you leave the door cracked for growth, not for reentry.

Begin with order. First, name what is true. Second, set or enforce the boundary. Third, apply the consequence that fits. Only then offer grace. This order keeps grace from becoming escape. It also keeps justice from turning into cruelty. Truth corrects. Boundaries protect. Consequences teach. Grace releases the grip that would keep everyone trapped inside a single moment.

Grace is quiet strength. It does not erase receipts. It does not remove accountability. It changes your posture toward the past. You stop rehearsing speeches in your head. You stop auditioning witnesses for your pain. You stop writing the same story every night. You choose peace as your permanent address, even as you keep the locks on your door.

At home, grace softens the air after repair. A child breaks a rule, cleans up, and practices the better way. End with a simple line that resets belonging. We are good. Try again tomorrow. Do not keep the offense on the table. Do not turn it into a nickname. Children grow steady when they are not defined by their worst moment.

With a partner, grace protects closeness after a conflict is resolved. You spoke the truth. You set a new plan. You both did your part. Now let the room breathe. Do not reopen the wound to win future points. If a memory rises, speak it as a fact without using it as a weapon. Then return to the present. Grace keeps love from becoming a courtroom.

In friendship, grace shows up as warm endings and clean pauses. If you are stepping back, you can wish someone well without writing their faults into the sky. Thank you for the season we shared. I am taking space now. When you forgive a friend, you still may change access. That is your boundary. Grace removes the sting from your tone. It lets you leave the story without leaving your values.

At work, grace looks like finishing strong after a miss has been addressed. You documented the slip. You set a plan. You met the new date. End the thread with a neutral summary and a thank you for repair. Do not circulate old screenshots for sport.

Do not seed gossip. When new information arrives, judge it fresh. People do better work in a culture that knows how to close a chapter.

Your body is part of grace. Resentment lives in muscles. It tightens the jaw and the throat. Before you close a hard moment, take one minute. Put both feet flat. Inhale for four counts. Hold for two. Exhale for six. Drop your shoulders one inch. On the exhale, release the need to be avenged. Keep the need to be safe. Grace rests best in a regulated body.

Language carries grace. Keep lines that are short and clear. I wish you well. We are complete. Thank you for doing your part. I am not reopening this. I forgive you and I am changing access. I forgive you and I am staying. Here is what that will look like. These sentences end loops. They are kind without confusion.

Grace is not the same as contact. You can bless someone and still block them. You can let go and still keep your distance. You can attend the same event without creating a scene. Grace serves your health and the health of the room. It is the calm decision to remove heat, not the careless decision to remove history.

There will be people who mistake grace for weakness. Correct the read once. I care about results and respect. We have addressed this. I am moving on. Then follow your plan. Repeat the boundary if it is tested. Do not add extra speeches. Your consistency will teach what your words cannot.

Grace includes how you speak to yourself. When you grow, do

not keep punishing the version of you that did not know yet. Name the lesson. Keep the boundary that protects it. Offer yourself the same closing line you would offer someone you love. I understand why I chose that then. I choose better now. I am done with the replay.

Online, grace keeps you from losing your day to a thread that will never end. Correct once with a source if it is safe. Mute, block, or leave. Do not search for the person at 1 a.m. to see if they responded. End with a clear note in your own log. I did my part. I am done. Your attention is a gift. Grace decides where not to spend it.

Grace can include restitution. If you caused harm, you apologize, repair, and then you stop asking for reassurance. You let the other person heal at their pace. You keep showing the change over time. You do not keep spilling guilt into their lap. Grace receives consequence with a steady back and keeps walking.

Practice a simple closing ritual. When a hard conversation ends, write three lines in a notebook. Here is the truth we named. Here is the boundary we set. Here is the blessing I choose. The blessing can be as small as May we rest or May we learn. Close the notebook. Drink water. Take a short walk. Your body will learn that closure is a place it can find on purpose.

If grief rises because the ending is real, let it. Grace does not deny feeling. It gives feelings a clean container so they do not spill into places that do not deserve them. Cry in the shower. Pray or sit in silence. Write a letter you do not send. Then return to your life and do one kind task in the present. Sweep a floor. Send a thank you. Fold a shirt. Small order helps grace hold.

Teach this law to children and teams by modeling it. Let people see you correct, set a boundary, follow through, and then stop. Let them hear you say we are not going to keep talking about this. We are going to live the new plan. Rooms become lighter when leaders end moments cleanly.

Let grace be the last move. Not the first move. Not the only move. The last move. End with dignity. Release what you do not need to carry. Keep the structure that guards your peace. Then step forward. The day opens. Your spirit stays light. And the people who move with you learn what strength feels like when it is kind.

Be Kind, Be Kind, Be Kind!

Remember the quote from the beginning of the book?
"There are three ways to ultimate success.
The first way is to be kind.
The second way is to be kind.
The third way is to be kind."
— Fred Rogers

Well, if you're not sure who Fred Rogers is, that is none other than the world famous Mr. Rogers from the popular TV series that ran for decades Mister Rogers Neighborhood! Rogers was a marvelous man, he believed Kindness is not only a feeling but it is a method you can practice on three levels that hold a life together when the day gets loud.

First, be kind to your Inner world.

Your energy teaches before you speak. A calm breath, soft eyes, steady posture, and a clear aim tell the room it is safe to think. Treat your body like the house your words live in. Water before coffee. Quiet windows that protect your focus. One sentence that sets your purpose. When you care for your inner world,

Law 12 becomes natural. When you protect your quiet windows, Law 29 holds on hard days. People feel your steadiness before they hear your plan.

Second, be kind in the moment.

Kindness is clarity and respect in action. It sounds like names spoken with care. It looks like listening until you can repeat the other person's point without a twist. It also looks like boundaries. Law 11 reminds us that kindness has shape. A clean no can be the kindest word in the room when it protects dignity and prevents resentment. Your line is exact and useful here: "Saying yes sir or yes mamn can completely change how a person views you." Courtesy phrases are switches. They lower threat and open ears. Use what fits the setting. Yes, sir. Yes, ma'am. Yes, Officer. Yes, Coach. Often a person's name is best. Yes, Ms. Rivera. Thank you, Malik. Respect in your words changes how your energy is received, while your boundaries keep your peace intact.

Third, be kind by design.

Kindness that lasts becomes structure. You return what you take. You give public credit. You choose repair over punishment. You build rooms where others can win. That is Law 30, Law 31, Law 27, and Law 39 working together. Design turns good intentions into reliable outcomes. Decisions are written. Roles are clear. Tools remove friction. Credit travels. When kindness becomes design, it outlives the moment and often outlives you.

A short scene to make it plain

You step into a tense lobby before a meeting. You breathe in for four, hold for two, and out for six. Shoulders drop. Kindness to self. You greet each person by name and set the aim in one sentence. Kindness in the moment. You capture decisions on a shared page with owners and dates. Kindness by design. The temperature drops because people can see the path.

When kindness is tested

Kindness is not a blank check. If a pattern harms you or others, stop feeding the loop. Law 14 calls you to redirect energy instead of wrestling with noise. Speak one calm boundary and move to process. I want a good outcome. I am not available for this tone. I will follow up in writing at two. Use consequences that teach rather than punish, then close with grace. Law 42 keeps your spirit light while the structure stays firm.

Simple ways to practice today

Say the name, then say thank you with one specific reason. Replace hurry with one clear next step. Pair a soft voice with a firm boundary in the same sentence. Bless what you want to grow and put it on the calendar. None of this is fancy. All of it is powerful.

Plant beyond your timeline

Kindness grows stronger when it stretches past your own calendar. Teach a skill. Label a drawer so no one has to ask twice. Write a checklist that prevents the next person from falling. Share a template. Make a clean introduction and step back. That is Law 41. It is love with a calendar.

Keep confidences and exit clean

Guard the stories people trust you with. Speak to safety when needed, and otherwise hold what is not yours to share. That is Law 35. When you must leave a room or a role, close the loop, return what you borrowed, speak one kind truth, and walk. That is Law 36. People will remember how you departed long after they forget the details.

Why this works

Attention is water, words are light, and boundaries are the garden walls. When you place attention on what should grow, speak with care, and keep the shape that protects your peace, people around you relax. Work improves. Homes breathe. Your name becomes a quiet promise.

Closing

These forty two laws began with a simple conviction. Kindness is control. Kindness is strategy. Kindness is power that does not need to shout. You learned to steady your inner world so your presence is safe. You learned to anchor the moment with clear words and respectful tone. You learned to turn kindness into design so good becomes easier tomorrow than it was today. You learned to forgive for your own freedom, to credit others in public, to repair rather than punish, to curate a circle that keeps you honest and warm, to plant for the future, to exit clean, to apologize like it matters, and at the end, to let grace be the last move.

Carry this into your day like a small, sturdy toolkit. Breath. Posture. Purpose. Name. Boundary. Plan. Blessing. Use them in kitchens, lobbies, classrooms, and calls. Use them when you win and when you miss. Use them for the people you love and the people who test you. The world may not always say your name for it. It will feel the shade.

Here's one final quote from Mr. Rogers and it's my favorite. "There's no person in the whole world like you, and I like you just the way you are."
— Mister Rogers

Be kind to your inner world. Be kind in the moment. Be kind by design. Then rest. You have done your part.

www.ingramcontent.com/pod-product-compliance
Lightning Source LLC
Chambersburg PA
CBHW020929090426
42736CB00010B/1084